The Shortest Skirt

To Judy.
Mother Superior
Sally Jude

The Shortest Skirt

❀

Sally J Jardine

ISBN-13: 9781537626017
ISBN-10: 1537626019

FOR LEVI,
WHO WAS NOT AFRAID OF ATHEISTS,
AND WHO TAUGHT ME THAT LUTHERANS CAN BE FUN.

*"What I have written here strains to be true
but nevertheless is not true enough.
Truth is anecdotes, narrative, the snug, opaque
quotidian."*

JOHN UPDIKE, SELF-CONSCIOUSNESS

Table of Contents

CHAPTER 1

———— ⚜ ————

Watching and Waiting

THE LAST DAY of my first life was also the hottest day of the summer. Lucky for us, the Lincoln Continental Papa drove had the most frigid air-conditioning. I sat looking out of the side window as he drove north on Dixie Highway until it turned into Western Avenue. The streets of my hometown, Tinley Park, Illinois, blended into the streets of the next small Chicago suburb: Oak Forest, and then Posen. Finally nine miles passed and we were in the town of Blue Island. In my stomach, it seemed like a flock of moths were rehearsing a classical ballet. Even so, I smiled with content. The flutters were caused by excitement, even anticipation, like I usually felt all day on Christmas Eve, not sadness or foreboding. I knew my entire life was heading for a change and it couldn't happen quickly enough for me. Mama wanted us to stop for a farewell ice cream cone but I just wanted to "get there." I just wanted to become a nun. I wanted to cut off all my curly, auburn hair and put on the starched black veil and the long black habit of the sisters who had been my teachers and almas maters for nine years of Catholic schooling. I wanted to have a wooden rosary clanking from my belt, and I wanted to slide my hands into the wide sleeves of the black serge habit and kneel in the candlelit chapel while sisters intoned the ethereal Latin chant. And the first step was climbing the stairs of the squat, brick Aspirancy House at Mother of Sorrows convent.

The Mantellate Sisters owned a square block of real estate on Western Avenue and 138th Street. There an old-fashioned, square brick home on the southwest corner. North of that they had built a grade school with an attached boarding house for young children. On the southeast corner of the parcel they had built a two–story convent of dark red brick, and on the northeast corner they managed to build a large and modern high school building with chemistry labs and a music wing. When I was a student there in the early sixties, we had graduating classes of 150 girls. Yes, all girls. I don't know how this small group of nuns, mostly from Italy, came up with the funds to erect all these buildings. I have seen some of the senior nuns in action, though, and they had the same skills that you see Bing Crosby demonstrating on the old millionaire in "Bells of Saint Mary." They had the persuasive powers of Torquemada. But in a nice way. Mother Evarista was especially good at finessing a donation out of ordinary folks who thought they were at the school for a Christmas program or a lovely spaghetti dinner. And many other nuns could help their friends and family to give money and services for God's work. Crates of chickens or vegetables, old but serviceable cars, trays of bakery goods, and of course, green cash flowed into the convent kitchen or the bursar's wallet from good and generous people who sincerely wanted to help the nuns in their work of educating children.

After 8th grade graduation, I mounted a blitzkrieg campaign against my poor mom and dad. Objective: allow me to enter the convent as an Aspirant in the Mantellate Sisters, Servants of Mary. I pleaded with Mama every day for permission to enter the convent, ambushing her in the kitchen to state my case and maybe get an assent from her while she was distracted with dinner matters or in the bathroom as she put on her lipstick and eyebrows before going to work the night shift at our family restaurant. Three other girls from my class had already entered the order as aspirants, and I was white-hot to join them. Mama and Papa said no, as most parents would if their thirteen-year-old wanted to make a life-changing decision. Papa said, "You're too young to know what you want to do with the rest of your entire life."

During the last years of grade school at St. George Elementary, Tinley Park, Illinois, I began to identify with the sisters who were our teachers. I loved the way they looked in their black, graceful habits, the way they smelled like starch and ironing, the way they worked so hard at teaching us and trying to make good people out of the raw material in their classrooms. Many Catholic students tell tales of the mean sisters and the awful punishments meted out. And sometimes they did suffer outright abuse from sick women who should not have been in a convent. My classmates and I certainly had our share of smacks with the ruler, but I always felt the sisters had our welfare at heart.

My grade school class had 56 children in one classroom. Some years that number went up or down a couple of kids, but being the sole adult in charge of 56 children for six hours a day is not a walk in the woods. Many times, especially in the higher grades, the sisters had to resort to the dreaded ruler. Two whacks – one on left hand, one on the right – were *de rigueur.* Some transgressions were worse than others, and involved a larger group of offenders. Then we would all have to stand by our desks, hands held out at waist level, palm up, and get the wooden punishing whack. Soon as you got your whack, you said "Thank you, S'ter," and you sat down in your desk so Sister could get to the next miscreant. I don't think any of us were resentful. We all knew that even if we weren't participating in this particular mischief, we had been involved in several others that had gone unfound and unpunished. From the shared grins and shaking up and down of sore hands grew an adolescent camaraderie: Us against the Establishment.

We girls seldom got into such troubles, but I did draw negative attention to myself in seventh grade. I had such a crush on the assistant priest at our parish. Father Gordon Campbell was tall and slim and much younger than our parish priest, the pudgy, waddling Father O'Connell. Father Campbell also had a bit of a Scottish brogue which bewitched my ears. I would be especially attentive when he said Mass, genuflecting more deeply and praying more fervently in hopes that he would see me and take note of that devout young girl in the congregation. One day he showed up at our school to give us seventh-graders a talk. I was giddy and excited when Sr. Virginia told us that Father Campbell was going to talk with us, first the girls and then the boys. That meant it would be about sex. No one separated the class unless the topic was sex.

"Good afternoon, boys and girls" he intoned while gliding into the stuffy classroom. It was after lunch and the scent of peanut butter sandwiches, apples, and milk hung in the air. Father Campbell stood at the front of the class, tall and smiling, black cassock still swirling gracefully around his hips. We rose as one unit, standing in the aisle by our desks, "Good afternoon, Father Campbell," we sing-songed back to him. He bade us sit and asked Sister to take the boys to the lunchroom for a study hall as he would like to speak to the girls.

I was bursting with anticipation and foreboding. I wanted to see him and hear him talk but I was afraid he would say something embarrassing. Being a redhead, my fair-skinned, freckled face came ablush at every passing emotion; any fleeting thought could bring a pink wash of color flowing upward from my neck to my forehead. Besides my personal interest in Father, he was going to talk to us girls about sex. A man talking to us about sex! I sternly willed myself not to turn red. Counterproductive, of course.

Father talked about boys and their needs – no one admitted that girls might also have needs - and how we must pray to the Blessed Virgin Mother to help us stay pure. No parts were named, and no actions explained so we ended up with not much more information than we started with. With a look of trust and sincerity, he told us that if we ever find ourselves in a situation with a boy, and somehow we no longer had our blouse on, we should be sure to have pinned on our bras a blue ribbon to remind us of the Blessed Mother and her purity. And that memory would make us strong enough to take charge of the moment and tell the boy that was as far as we would go. No further.

My God, Father Campbell said the word "bra" in front of us all. And he thinks we are going to take off our white cotton blouses in front of a boy. How embarrassing and how thrilling to think we might do that. Steadily and without my consent, the burning red tide kept rising in my face. I bent my face down toward the desk, fanning my cheeks with a black marbled notebook, putting cool fingers on them. Nothing made a dent in this volcano of redness and heat. Finally Father Campbell turned his soulful dark eyes toward me and asked, "Miss Jardine, do you need a drink of water?"

"Yes, Father; thank you, Father" I mumbled and slithered out of the room to the water fountain in the hall. Once out of his sight, I leaned against the wall and took deep breaths. Triumph! Glory! Father Campbell spoke to me! He knew my name! All that genuflecting and extra prayers after Mass had paid off.

Sister Virginia brought the boys up from the lunchroom then and we switched places, girls to the lunchroom, boys in the classroom for their talk. Some of the girls told Sister about me turning a hundred shades of red and said that I had a crush on Father Campbell. Sister swiveled her starched black-veiled and white-wimpled head toward me and made the "meet me in the hall" motion. Once again I slithered out the door into the hallway, this time with fear instead of triumph in my heart. Sister followed me out and delivered a short but emphatic talk about how unbecoming and inappropriate my actions were in a young girl and how shameful it was to have impure thoughts about a priest – a priest! - how she had expected much better from me, and how ashamed Blessed Mother Mary was over my immodesty and my pursuit of a priest – a priest!. And how I had just better quit this right this instant.

"Yes, S'ter," I muttered. And we both went back into the classroom, my face crimson yet again.

Our class was moving toward graduation. Chubby Checker had been singing about The Twist, and I learned how to do it by practicing at Diane Ziska's house. Diane and I twisted and gyrated for hours with the record player cranked up as loud as possible. Our pattern for the dances we practiced was Dick Clark's American Bandstand Show. Boy and girl parties were held in family basements and I prevailed upon my mom and dad to let me have a dance party for my birthday. It was a cool September evening. The kids brought records and danced to "Mrs. Brown You've Got a Lovely Daughter" and "Wooly Bully". We slow danced to Brenda Lee's "I'm Sorry" and Paul Anka's "Lonely Boy," and to those sexy Righteous Brothers' "Unchained Melody." My main objective was to slow dance with Tommy Bockstahler. He was very sweet, as were most of the boys in my class, but he was also very shy – like me. I didn't know how to make him ask me, so I started dancing with Gary Berner, another redhead and a good guy who just liked to dance. Somehow, the lights went off momentarily, and in the confusion, Gary and I ended up behind a partition wall. Tommy looked around for me and got a little upset that I was missing. Sighting me and Gary, he came over and tapped Gary on the shoulder, asking for the dance. The radio started up again with "Tell Laura I Love Her." Cheek to cheek with Tommy had been my goal, but once there, I was uneasy and pulled away as soon as the song ended. Too close and too scary. I rushed over to the refreshment table and mumbled something about going up to the kitchen to get more Cokes. Tommy watched my flight up the stairs with a bewildered look on his face.

Our school had always sent the classes on field trips in May. As third-graders, we went to the Chicago Museum of Science and Industry and spent lots of time looking at the huge miniature railroad, watching chicks break out of their eggshells, and pressing all the interactive buttons on every display. On alternate years, we would be taken to the Museum of Natural History or the Science and Industry or the Art Institute. But since eighth-graders are special, there was always a bigger class trip planned for them.

Our class trip was to Starved Rock State Park. We bussed up there in late May, when the teachers could hardly stand to keep us in the classroom anymore. Starved Rock State Park is a rocky landscape of sandstone cliffs and noisy waterfalls near Utica, about seventy miles west of our town. Our bus ride going up was filled with long-distance songs like "99 Bottles of Beer on the Wall" and "My Gal's A Corker, She's a New Yorker." Once there, we were given the lecture on behaving like young Catholic adults, and told when and where to meet for lunch. Then we were cast free to roam and climb the cliffs and inhale nature.

Groups formed of six to eight friends, girls and boys together. We climbed and clambered everywhere. Some slide down the rocks and scrapped knees, but mostly we had a wonderful time.

Young Sister Daniel hung out with the group I was in. Sr. Daniel was tall and thin and boyish. She walked with a tilt, like a sailor, her habit swaying behind her. She was great at lunchtime baseball and good at keeping the boys in line, knocking them in the arm and giving them lots of attention. She formed a choir and rehearsed the girls in two-part singing. We all loved her. We felt she loved us back.

Sister Daniel and I were working our way down a pretty steep path, trying not to slide down the hillside. The others in our group were way down the hill below us, bunched together on an outcropping boulder where the river could be seen rushing by. A little drizzle had started to fall on us even though the sun was still bright.

"Sister, your veil is going to get wet. All your starch will melt," I said to her, worried that she would get in trouble if she returned to school with her habit messed up.

"Well, I will just have to take it off if that happens, Sally," she replied airily, with a wink.

"Take it off? You can't do that – we would see your hair. You're a nun!" I answered in alarm.

"Sally dear, the veil does not make the nun. My vows to Jesus make me his spouse, and my commitment to the work he sends me makes me a religious. Being a nun is not about the clothes we wear. It's about making a choice to serve God in whatever place he sends us," she said. "I would still be a nun even if you saw my hair," she said as she rubbed the top of my head which the rain and humidity had turned into a red spaghetti mop.

"Sister, I thought you didn't have any choice about being a nun. I thought that God chose you. And you had to do it, or maybe you would get struck down dead," I countered.

"Yes and no, honey," she said. "God does call us; he chooses us to be his servants in this world and to carry his good news to his people. He calls each of us to come be his bride, but we are free to tell God 'Forget it' or 'Leave me alone'. We don't have to say yes. But, Sally, when you say yes to God, immediately you have the sweetest peace in your heart, and you receive the counsel and guidance of the Holy Spirit – it's like he is sitting on your shoulder and showing you the way to go. And you never have to worry again about what to do, what to wear, how to find a job, or a husband. All this is now in God's hands. Once you say 'Yes,' everything else is so simple," she smiled and raised her brows at me as if she had just given me the answer to the riddle of life.

We had by then wormed our way down the slope to the gathering place on the boulder and our time to talk was over for now.

"Who's ready for lunch?" Sister Daniel asked the kids. The boys all said they were, and we girls were hungry, too, although we wouldn't say so in front of the guys.

All the way home on the bus I looked out the window at the passing roadway while these new ideas buzzed around in my head. Against the backdrop of chatter and dramatic recounting of the day's events: rainstorm and lost and found friends and bug bites and slips and slides on the rocky paths, I was lost in my thoughts. So I don't have to wait for a sign. I can just tell the nuns that I think God wants me to be a nun, and they will have to let me in? I didn't have to worry about boys or dances or kissing or blue ribbons on my bra. I could be the Bride of Christ and leave all the rest behind me.

Three other girls in my eighth-grade class had the same idea, and their parents gave them permission to enter the aspirancy at Mother of Sorrows convent in August after graduation: Nancy Czernik, Carol Burklow, and my best friend, Colette Wagner. Each applied and were admitted to the Servite Order. All three got busy in the weeks after graduation as they purchased and packed the items on the list given them by the Aspirant Mistress, Sr. Marguerite. White cotton nightgowns – long-sleeved – were on the list. Six under-shirts, six cotton underpants, two pair of sensible, low-heeled black shoes, six pair of stockings, a dozen handkerchiefs, a rosary, any spiritual books you might wish, a statue or two of Mary or Jesus to place on your nightstand, any medications you needed. What was definitely off the list, though important to a thirteen-year-old girl: purses, scarves, jewelry of any sort, hair ribbons or barrettes, records or record players, autograph books, lipstick, hairspray, mas-cara, letters from old boyfriends or pictures of same. One could bring a photo of their immediate family, but just one. As soon as the aspirant had collected all these necessities, she stowed then away in a trunk, or foot locker, which would be her only personal posses-sions during her aspirancy. As my friends shopped and discussed the various brands and prices of their gathered goods, I felt less and less a part of their plans.

"I'll probably be joining up next year," I told them.

"Yeah, as soon as your mom and dad say yes, come talk to Sr. Marguerite. She will get you a list and all the paperwork and a uni-form," Nancy told me. And they started discussing again the type of undershirts she had found at JC Penny's.

My parents were, of course, upset about the idea of me leaving home at age thirteen. Hindsight tells me they were right to make me wait, knowing that I was a very young thirteen, and a late-bloomer who was quite suggestible. I followed easily whenever someone had an idea, and I was not noticeably religious. During Mass, I always lost interest after about ten minutes. The singing was the main reason I liked church, the singing in Latin, and the gold embossed censors swinging on long chains with fragrant smoke curling up and out, over the congregation. I liked the paintings on the walls, the statue of Saint Joseph holding a carpenter's square in one hand and the child Jesus on his other arm. The high ceilings, the candles, the colorful panoply of the seasons of the church, the vestment changes from green to red to white to purple as the liturgical year makes its inevitable round – all that theatre drew me in. I liked the bowing and genuflecting of the priest, mirrored by the congregation. Most of all, I liked the mysterious Latin chants and prayers. Our missals had the left side printed in English to translate the right side which was Latin. Translating gave me something to do while the interminable prayers moved on. The vocabulary of religion is narrow, mostly please give and forgive us and grant us peace and how mighty and merciful thou art so it was easy to learn the Latin basics. And it was easy for an unsophisticated child to fall under the spell of the Catholic drama, forgetting to examine my true motives when I said I wanted to be a part of the church.

Since the parents would not budge on this issue, I took the second-best course and begged them to let me go to high school at Mother of Sorrows as a regular student. There was a nice Irish girl in our town who was a senior at MOS, and my folks paid her to take me with as she drove to school every day. That was a lucky break. I hung around with the three aspirants from my grade school and continued my assault on Mama and Papa daily, whining (so they say, I don't remember any whining) and begging them to please let me be a nun.

Finally, Mama said, "Ralph, she has become so hard to live with, grim and cranky all the time. Maybe we should let her go live with the sisters. At least we won't have to worry about her driving out late with boys, maybe drinking, maybe getting pregnant. She'll be safe there. And if she doesn't like it, she can come right home."

Papa eventually agreed, and in April, I happily started gathering my own foot locker full of undershirts and white cotton nightgowns. All summer I shopped and compared notes with my aspirant friends, and when August 23rd arrived, the feast day of St. Philip Benizi who was one of the founding fathers of the Servite Order back in the thirteenth century, Papa drove me and Mama and Grandma Anna to the Motherhouse. There I would be received into the order as the lowliest of the lowly. A brand new aspirant is the very bottom of the pecking order in religion.

CHAPTER 2

The Goodbye Blues

No one ever forgets their first day in religion. A chasm opens between the secular and the religious world and you have to take your courage in your hands and tread carefully across the one-way bridge between the two worlds.

Dressed in Sunday clothes, my parents and grandmother stood awkwardly in the reception hall, a large space filled with groupings of unmatched, donated chairs and tables. Each table had a small vase in the middle with a fistful of plastic blooms. Later this would seem sad to me, but right now I was ready to say goodbye to the world and move into my new life. Nancy Czernik was returning for her second year, Katherine Macdonald, Lois Sowalski, Colette Wagner also. Pretty Carol Burklow did not return. She went home after spring semester, deciding this was not her vocation after all. Every year there is attrition, either voluntary or forced, among the aspirant population. Besides myself, there were two other new girls coming in as freshmen: Denise Fleming, and Margaret McNamara, both standing around with their families, chatting uncomfortably with the welcome party of nuns.

Mother Evarista was our order's highest ranking nun in America, our Mother Superior. She was very short, olive-skinned, with heavy dark eyebrows that showed her mood whenever someone acted badly. Sister Marguerite, thin and pale, was the Aspirant Mistress. She moved from one family group to the next, making all welcome. Her glance was sharp and even then, I thought, critical of each of us. Sisters whose names I didn't yet know offered us squares of sheet cake and little glasses of red juice that I later learned was Tamarindo, made from a paste of the tamarind pod, sweet and tart at the same time. I came to like Tamarindo very well, but this day I was too nervous to taste anything. I talked distractedly with my family about little nothings and future visiting times until Sister Marguerite came over to us and introduced herself. Mama asked when she should come next to visit, and Sister Marguerite explained about Visiting Sunday being on the first Sunday of the month. Family was allowed to visit in this very same hall from 2 PM to 5 PM. Since this was August 23rd, Visiting Sunday was two weeks away. That thought made everyone feel a little better about driving away and leaving their daughters.

Finally, Mother Evarista nodded to Sister Marguerite, who clapped her hands and said it was time for the young women to enter God's House. She thanked the parents for being generous and giving their dear daughters into the convent's care, and asked us girls to say our goodbyes and come line up at the inner doorway where she and Mother Evarista were standing.

I hugged my grandma first. She slipped a pearly rosary into my hand and said to be good and to pray for her. Mama was silent when we hugged. No tears, but she had a hanky squeezed in her left hand, just in case. Papa surprised me by being the one with tears. He squeezed real hard, and I said we would see each other on Visiting Sunday. He slipped a twenty dollar bill into my hand, "just in case you need something and they don't have it here," he said.

I saw Sr. Marguerite bend toward Denise and speak into her ear. Then Denise turned red and slipped a little silver ring off her finger and hurried after her mom and dad, giving them the ring to take home with them. I had no rings or earrings, just a graduation watch – Bulova, not fancy. Watches seemed to be acceptable.

After all the siblings and grandparents and parents finished their goodbyes, we girls moved over toward the inner door. We were lined up in our order of entry: Katherine, Lois, Nancy, Colette, and then me, Denise, and Margaret. Our Mistress opened the paneled oak door, and with equal parts of joy and fear, I walked into the next seven years of my life.

Still in an orderly line, we walked to the Aspirant house, into the parlor where we were out of the public view, and received, one by one, the tools of the craft: The Little Office of the Blessed Virgin Mary, a rosary if we had none, and a copy of the Rulebook. These three items were to be treasured and guarded, not given up to the eyes of the public, especially the Rulebook. Our lives would now be governed by the teachings of the Seven Holy Founders of the Servite Order and by the canonical hours of the Little Office. Most convents prayed using the Little Office of the Blessed Virgin Mary, instead of following the daily hours in the Breviary that all the priests used. Our office was shorter, perhaps because nuns are always working in schools or hospitals and had less time for prayer and meditation than priests did. We each said, "Thank you, Sister," as the items were placed in our hands. Inwardly, I vowed to try harder than anyone to be worthy of the rule and the Little Office.

Next we went upstairs to the dormitory and were assigned our places. Since it was now after five o'clock, we didn't linger to put away our clothes, but instead went straight to chapel to say the evening prayers. Sister Marguerite showed us the page in the Little Office where the prayers would begin and gave us each a holy card to mark the place. Then we hurried down the stairs and across the lawn to the chapel inside the high school building where the fading sunlight through the tall, gold and blue windows of the chapel covered the nuns with celestial splendor. Many sisters had already filed into the chapel and were in their accustomed places. As the youngest members, we were sent to the front pews. I worried how we would know when to stand or kneel, but Sister Marguerite took her place at the end of our row, so I kept a close watch on her and did as she did, with a second delay.

If I was feeling blue or homesick, here the cure was presented to me. Clear soprano voices intoning the Latin Vespers, bowing their heads at the name of Jesus, their bridegroom, kneeling with straight backs and raised heads as the verses rolled upward like ribbons of incense. There was no organ playing, only the song of the virgins keeping watch. I was entranced by the antique beauty of those chanted prayers that first night and truly, the Canonical Hours- Matins, Lauds, Prime, Terce, Sext, None, Vespers and Compline— never lost their power over me. Every day the verses changed but the structure stayed the same. All of us tried hard to follow and move to the correct pages. We fumbled over the Latin and glanced left and right at each other's book for clues. Then I just stopped flapping pages and stood still, letting the sound roll over my head. All was beauty, lit with the last golden shards of light. And I was sure, as time passed, that I would get this right. Tonight was a night for savoring where I was – in the convent. In an actual convent after all those months of pleading. How medieval the moment felt. The same exact words and tones had been sung for centuries and now I was participating in an ancient ritual. This would be my life. Yes, and amen.

After prayers we followed Sr. Marguerite to the refectory for our first supper. Our tables were set in a small alcove, separate from the nuns' large, tile-floored refectory. We could hear them and see some of them, but there was a sliding double door that could be closed when privacy was needed for the sisters.

We were assigned places at the table and kept the same for all three years of our aspirancy unless someone should leave. Then the next would move upward. Each place had a drawer with silverware and a white cloth napkin. Neatness was requisite because you only got a clean napkin every Sunday. All sisters and aspirants stood behind their chairs and waited for Mother Evarista to give the signal to proceed. The sister whose turn it was to be reader intoned the prayer for grace, and we joined in; then we all sat.

More chair noise was produced by our group than by all the professed sisters. We had to learn to move chairs out quietly, no scraping and dragging.

While we ate, a sister read to us from a suitable book: lives of the saints or anything that the superior thought would be educational and exemplary. I was surprised that we had to keep silent. I looked over at Nancy and she nodded to me. Nancy and Colette already knew this from last year.

The sisters on kitchen duty brought out the platters of food. The head of each table, in our case Sr. Marguerite, took her portion and then passed the platter to the next sister. My curiosity was soon filled as I saw white bread and bologna sandwiches and some kind of soup being passed, and bread and butter, and since tonight was a special occasion – new aspirants arriving – we had a dessert also: Hostess snowballs and Twinkies and those Hostess chocolate cupcakes with the white squiggle. Each of the professed sisters took one and bit into it with gusto. We Aspirants, so lately of the world, were not all that excited about the goodies, but we also took our portion. I could see that this was a special treat and not likely to happen very often so I enjoyed my Twinkie. I learned later that the treats were always a donation from some store. The convent would never spend money on extravagances like Twinkies. And as another treat, Mother announced that we may all chat for a while as we ate our dessert. She told the sisters that there were several new aspirants tonight – as if they hadn't already seen that – and they should come visit us and meet their new little sisters.

Many of the sisters did walk over to our alcove, asking Sr. Marguerite who her new charges were. She introduced us and told us the name of each visitor. "This is Sr. Chiarina; she is our habitor and will make your new school uniforms, and this is Sr. Floriana who helps her with the sewing. This is Sr. Ernesta; she is Mother's driver and she gets up very early and goes into Chicago to the market to get our produce and supplies. This is Sr. Raphael; she is in charge of the boys at the boarding school. And this is Sr. Mary; she is our receptionist and door keeper."

Sr. Chiarina was smiling, nodding, and silent. Sr. Floriana was a lively, dark-eyed Italian woman with wildly moving eyebrows. She nodded at us and let loose a flood of Italian commentary to Ernesta about our hair and clothes and worldly manners. Floriana could speak some English but didn't like to. Sr. Ernesta was a solid woman. She also peppered us with Italian exclamations mixed with questions in English about where our families lived, and what streets did we come down to get to the convent. Since she was the driver, she knew the best way to get anywhere in the South Side. She looked capable of hefting a crate of fruit or vegetables up on her shoulder and carting it to the back of the station wagon. Sr. Rafael was tall and slim and her eyes cut from side to side, taking in every movement. This was probably the reason they put her in charge of the boys. She missed nothing. She looked like she could beat anyone at basketball. I thought the boarding school boys must like her. Her manner was rough but I learned she worked and worried over the kids in her care. Sr. Mary was not a sister, she was an adoptee. She was about 4'6", chubby, and elderly, a woman who would not be able to keep a job in the world. Her mother had been a benefactor of the convent and before she died, she begged the sisters to take Mary and give her a home. Mary waddled down the hall whenever the doorbell rang. As she passed, you heard her mumbling and talking to herself. Sometimes the boarding school children would say unkind things to her and she would get very distressed and cry and go tell Mother. She would find some comfort there for her bruised feelings.

Several of our high school teachers came in and said hello. It was about two weeks before the start of school and it felt strange to be sort of related to them now, instead of just being one of their students. Lastly, we met Sr. Addolorata and Sr. Antoinette, our cooks. They both entered our alcove in their white cooking habits. Short and bent-backed, Addolorata smiled and nodded at us with true kindness in her face and welcomed us warmly, mostly in English, but with a little Italian mixed in. Antoinette was a Celtic figure, slender, pale skin, pale brows and eyelashes– I was sure she had red hair although I couldn't see any of it. Looking us over disparagingly, she tossed her head at us and told Marguerite that she certainly had her work cut out for her if she planned to turn us into proper sisters. I guess our chair scraping was audible in the kitchen. Nancy politely complimented the cooks on our dinner, but Antoinette was not to be won over easily. She sailed straight-backed out of the refectory, the two ends of her veil filled with air like a ship's canvas. She turned her head back toward us and said, over her shoulder, "Marguerite, be sure to show them how to wash their silverware before they put it away." And she was gone.

I blinked, surprised that sisters were allowed to have personalities like that. Sr. Marguerite was always calm and helpful. Antoinette's dramatic flair was something I had never seen in a nun. I would see definitely see more of it in other nuns.

Sister Marguerite gathered us together and showed us where to take our dishes and glasses, and where to go to wash our silverware at a little sink in one corner of the refectory, dry them and put them back into the our drawers for the next meal. She hurried us along like a mother hen, saying "Move a little faster, girls. We will be late for chapel." And back to chapel we trooped for Compline and the rosary. Thirty minutes of chanting and standing and kneeling, entering the arcane drama, put me back into a serene mood.

My euphoria from the singing of the Hours evaporated after I got into my nightgown and got in bed. Our dormitory was really two bedrooms on the second floor of the Aspirancy. Sr. Marguerite, of course, had her own room. The rest of us were divided into two large rooms. We had beds pushed against each wall, so eight could be accommodated easily. Only one bathroom proved to be a bit harder. We developed a rotation for showering or tubbing that worked alright. Changing clothes modestly was difficult until the experienced girls showed us newbies how to pull our white nightgowns over our heads and then take off our skirts and blouses and underthings without being exposed. Since the nightgowns were voluminous, this plan worked great. Eventually, our ablutions were finished. Heads were laid upon pillows and the long summer sunset turned to darkness. Some sniffles were heard. And then, quiet.

CHAPTER 3

---·❧·---

As the Reed is Bent

Sr. Marguerite did indeed have her work cut out for her, as Antoinette said. Here were six girls, 14 and 15 years old, who must be prepared for life as religious women.

Morning arrives early in the convent. 5:30 in the summer months; 6:30 in the winter. When the bell rings, God's servant jumps out of bed with a willing heart, falls to her knees next to her bed, and begins the day with prayer. "Benedicamus Domine," the bell ringer intones.

"Deo gratias," we all answer. Let us bless the Lord, and thanks be to God. Dressing, morning ablutions, and a brisk walk to the chapel place us back in that ethereal atmosphere of slanting sunlight, this time from the East windows, and the susurrations of the robes of the rising and bowing sisters, and the comforting intonations of the Latin chant.

After breakfast, I wondered what we would do all day. Would we have to pray for hours? Maybe do this in shifts – two hours praying, two hours off?

What we actually would do was clean. Six new workers had just entered the order and the order used them well. After breakfast, we went to the boarding school and were assigned areas of our own to clean. Lois got the parlor, an easy job in my estimation since it was all furniture and a piano and little rugs. It was a large room but not often used, so not much dirt could accumulate. Colette got the refectory, our dining hall, but she was only to clean the Aspirant's side, not the professed sister's side. That was kept private from us.

We only entered there if we were invited. Denise was assigned the bathrooms and the little parlor where the sisters served breakfast to Father Lambert after he said Mass for us.

Nancy got to help the sacristan. I was so envious. Sacristan is the sister who takes care of all the linen and candles and various appointments for the altar. The green and white and red chasubles that the priest wears for Mass were in her care, as well as the gold or silver-plated vessels used for communion, and the censors that burned incense during Benediction. Arranging flowers for the altar and keeping the sanctuary lamp lit were part of the sacristan's duties. There would be a little dusting and moping of the floors, but most of the work was clean and fragrant and I wanted to do it. That was the first sin of the day: Envy.

My assignment was stairs, three flights of five foot wide terrazzo stairs at the administration building/boarding school. I thought it would be a snap when I heard the assignment. I could start at the top with a broom and be done in ten minutes. That's what I did, and I returned to the aspirant house, expecting to read a book for the rest of the time before lunch. Sr. Marguerite came into the room and saw me reading the novel assigned for sophomore English, "Catcher in The Rye." Margaret was upstairs cleaning her assignment: the bedrooms and bathroom.

"Sally, what are you doing here? Aren't you supposed to be cleaning at the boarding school?" she asked me.

"I'm all done, Sister. I'm reading my book for English class," was my artless reply.

"You swept and washed three flights of stairs in fifteen minutes?"

"Well, I swept them all. They didn't look very dirty. I don't think they need to be washed this week," I proffered over my shoulder, and turned back to my book. The second sin: Disobedience.

Sister picked the book out of my hand. She motioned me to stand up out of the chair and looked straight into my eyes. "Our rule doesn't ask us to think. It asks us to be obedient to the directions that our superiors give us, and to accept their direction in all things," she instructed me. "Now go back to the boarding school and sweep the steps again and wash them with the bucket and brush that I pointed out to you. Hurry, so you will not be late for lunch." She said it in a kindly but firm voice. I knew there was no room for negotiations here.

"Yes, sister. Thank you, Sister," I replied, bobbing up and down, and fleeing down the steps toward the boarding school.

So back I trudged to the cleaning closet and grabbed the broom and the scrub brush and some rags, and filled the bucket with water. Climbing to the top of the stairs, three flights up, I started to sweep. After the upper flight was swept – for the second time that day - I knelt down on the third step and scrubbed the grey-green terrazzo with the brush, and dried off the water with the rags. Every three steps I had to descend to a lower level and set up my bucket and rags. Thirty-nine stairs and three large landings were sparkling clean when the bell rang to signal lunch would soon be served and I rose from the landing floor and massaged my aching knees. How often would this have to be done, I wondered? Once a month?

Lunch was nearly ready. It smelled wonderful and the scent had been rising up the stairwell for the last forty minutes so I was so ready to eat. I stopped in the bathroom to wash my hands, and smooth down my hair. And there was Denise, on her knees, scrubbing around the bottom of a toilet with a little brush. Her springy dark hair was exploding around her face from the dampness of the work and from perspiration. Sunshine from the four tall windows made the room hot and all her scrubbing made it moist.

"Are you finished yet, Denise? It's almost lunch time," I asked.

"I was finished but Sr. Marguerite came by and said that I didn't clean the toilets good enough, and she gave me this little brush so that I could get in all the cracks between the toilets and the floor. " She wiped her arm across her forehead.

"What else needs doing?" I asked.

"Well, I did the sinks already. Could you wipe off the mirrors and fill the soap dispensers? Then I'll be done."

We both stared for a moment at the very clean bathroom, and then at each other. If this was not good enough, how would we ever know what was good enough? I got to work polishing the mirrors. When the final bell rang for lunch, we put away our cleaning gear, not at all convinced that we wouldn't have to get the stuff out and clean everything all over again. I had been raised in a clean home, and had my Saturday chores that had to be completed, but this convent cleaning was way beyond anything I had ever seen.

Chicken and spaghetti for lunch! That's what that wonderful aroma creeping up the stairs had been. What a delicious reward for all that work.

After our silent lunch, we were herded outside for recreation. Many of the older sisters just sat around on outdoor chairs and benches. I could see an area set up for horseshoes. The younger sisters wanted to move so they set up the volleyball net and invited the new aspirants to join the game. Not being a sporty girl, I was reluctant to join but it seemed to be required, so I stood on one side of the net with Denise and Lois and three of the nuns. Nancy and Colette and Margaret joined the other side. When the ball came toward me, I dangled my hand out in front on me and tried to shove it back toward the other team. Sr. Joseph, lean and very aggressive, said, "Sally, what's wrong with you? Get up front by the net. Hit that ball."

I shrugged and moved closer to Denise. She seemed to know what to do. Denise returned the ball several times, diving over into my area twice. "When it comes to you, just get under it and slam it back over the net," she advised, "Make a fist and whack the ball back over the net."

How I got to sophomore year without playing team sports was the result of a deliberately planned strategy on my part. Whenever there was talk of a team sport, I volunteered to stay inside and help distribute the milk to the little kids' classes, or help Sister arrange a new bulletin board. Anything to get out of physical activities. Freshman year I took Glee Club twice so there would be no way to schedule gym class. And our girls' school didn't really have much in the way of sports. We had folk dancing where you danced in a square with four or eight dancers. There were a few intramural basketball or volleyball teams but I steered clear of them. Now I was stranded in a situation where I had to smack volleyballs into the faces of nuns! What was I supposed to do?

Back and forth the ball flew. Sr. Martina was short but she moved fast. She spiked the ball from the opposition's back row. It was flying right toward my face. I raised my arm in front of my face to ward off the ball. At the same time, Sr. Joseph launched herself toward me from our back row. She could tell that I wasn't going to slap the ball back across the net. As I turned to my left to deflect the ball, she came rushing toward the net, right arm extended. She slammed the ball with the heel of her hand. Her momentum made her fall onto me and we both collapsed into a heap on the grass. The mothball smell of her habit was in my face. Her rosary was hanging over my nose. Her skinny arms and her boney torso were pinning me to the ground. She jumped up immediately and started to brush the grass and dirt off her skirts, laughing. "Jardine, you are pitiful," she said. "Don't you have eyes in your head? You just stood there like a statue of Saint Stephan, pierced by arrows!"

Blushing madly, I just kept my eyes on the ground. So much actual bodily contact with a nun was hard for me to process. We had been taught never to touch a nun. All through grade schools we learned to pull on sister's sleeve if we wanted her attention. No one ever touched sister's hand or arm. And now I had been completely buried by a nun. Was that a sin? Did I need to confess?

Mother Evarista rose from her lawn chair and signaled that recreation was over. A wash of relief swept over me. The third sin: Cowardice.

CHAPTER 4

First Formation Days

NOW CAME THE time of instruction. Sr. Marguerite lead us all back to the large table in the aspirant house. In a regular house it would be a dining table in a dining room, but since we ate in the refectory, this table was where we would spend many hours studying and doing our homework. This afternoon was spent listening to a short history of the Servite Order. The Order was started 1233 in Florence by seven young men, sons of the patrician merchant houses who wanted to give their lives to prayer and good works. The niece of one of these men wanted to serve God in this same way, and she started the women's branch of the Servite order, called Mantellate Sisters, around 1285. We learned the origin of our "letters", the O.S.M. that we would one day be able to write after our names. The letters stood for "Ordo Servorum Beatae Mariae Virginis", Order of the Servants of the Blessed Virgin Mary. In English, we simply said, Order of the Servants of Mary. As aspirants, we were not allowed to use the designation. Later, after we made our first Profession, we would proudly write O.S.M. after our religious names.

Sr. Marguerite had several small and medium-sized books about the Order and the Seven Holy Founders. She gave each of us one of them, and told us to spend some time reading about those who had suffered and died so that we could become Mantellates. There was nothing I liked better than reading so I dove right into the stories of St. Juliana Falconieri and her struggles with her family. She also had a hard time getting them to let her go. I identified with that.

Denise's book was about the Seven Holy Founders and she really took to heart the story of Amadeus Amadei, who was pictured as a young and handsome – and blonde – Italian lad. She started pestering Sr. Marguerite for a relic of Amadeus to put on her nightstand.

A relic is a piece of hair or bone of a sainted person, or even a piece of the clothing or some other thing that was touched by that person, Usually these are mounted on a card or in a frame and are held to be not sacred, but memorable because the object brings that person to mind. In some ways, it's like your mother keeping your old baby shoes. If you have a relic you can focus your prayers or thoughts on that person more easily than you can if you are just staring into space. So, Denise was adamant about finding a relic of Amadeus. Myself, I think she really just liked saying his name, Amadeus Amadei. She and I were the only Italians girls in our group, and we were both at least one generation removed from full Italian-ness. I was two levels down from real Italian-ness. Mama was half Italian, half Swedish, and I was that from her and an Appalachian mix of English, Scottish, maybe French from my father's side but since my Italian grandma had lived with us since I was four, I had been schooled in the language and the lore, and I felt quite at home with the Servite Order. I myself had a rather dubious relic of St. Teresa of Avila, a piece of her mantel, and was therefore quite interested in Denise's relic quest.

Now, these relics were not very large. One does not want to squander the holy remains on just a few, so your regular relic is hardly bigger than a peppercorn. My piece of Teresa's mantel was the size of several of my freckles put together, but it was under a window of cellophane and mounted on a holy card with a prayer to St. Teresa surrounding it in lovely script. On the other side of the card was a reproduction of the wonderful and troubling *Ecstasy of Saint Theresa*, a disquieting statue by Bernini that always excited my adolescent imagination. Nancy Czernik had a relic, also, of St.

Stanislaus, a sickly young Polish boy who died trying to become a Jesuit. There was always a healthy trade in relics of saints afoot, so Sr. Marguerite told Denise she would see what she could do.

The bell rang, and time for chapel put an end to our spiritual reading. We donned our black mantillas, a small circle of lacey fabric that we bobby-pinned to our hair to cover our heads, as St. Paul said all women must. We hurried across the walk to the chapel and spent the next thirty minutes wrapped in Latin chant and candlelight.

The days went by quickly with prayer time, work time, spiritual reading time, and plenty of cleaning time. Some mornings were spent working in the high school library with Sr. Phillip. We helped shelve the books and polish the large oak tables. We quickly learned to put something under our spiral notebooks because Sr. Phillip was not going to have spiral scratches on her oak tables. Library duty was almost as good as sacristan duty. Clean and warm, we got relief from our dishwater hands when we pulled library rotation. We also got a chance to look through magazines. There were no *Cosmopolitans* or *Vogues*, but *National Geographic* was on the table, and *Catholic Digest*, *Time*, and *Newsweek* and the glossy photos in *Look*. Sometimes we had time to flip through the pages and see what was happening in the world. There were televisions in the community rooms of the convent but they were seldom turned on The teaching sisters would often gather there to look at the six o'clock or ten o'clock news so they would be prepared for anything their classes might want to talk about. The rest of us were not to watch. There was nothing in the world that we needed. When we used the library as a homework room, Sr. Phillip would come up behind us as we sat at the magazine table and would check what we were reading, making sure we weren't looking up photos of those frighteningly popular rock and roll singers. "These magazines are here to inform our students about political and spiritual issues. Any young woman aspiring to be a sister should use them only as needed for her studies, and not for recreational purposes," Sr. Phillip would tell us.

We also spent our non-cleaning time in the high school office helping Sr. Assuntina get the records in order for the incoming classes. Registration of the incoming class was in progress and Sister had forms for every possible necessity: family information, payment schedules, health exams, emergency contact info, gym suit order forms, and class schedules. The freshman class would probably number 160 or more young women and there were no computers to help with the work, just Sr. Assuntina and her inborn sense of organization. Denise and Margaret and I were sent to the first floor entry of the high school to set up tables for the textbook distribution. We lugged many cartloads of history, science, algebra, civics, religion, Latin, Spanish, French, German and home economics books to the entrance and opened boxes and put the books on the table under the Marine-sergeant direction of Sr. Concetta, typing teacher. Tall and skinny, she was a bundle of supervisory energy; she swooped around the hall like a South American condor in search of any aspirant moving too slowly, or worse, sitting down and resting. A boney hand would grasp your shoulder and turn you from your resting place so you could view the piles of unopened boxes.

"Do you think we are ready to stop work, young lady, and wait for you to put up your dainty feet and nap a little? How will all these textbooks get sorted out if we all are going to sit around chattering like squirrels?" Concetta blared. Eventually we learned that she was a good-hearted woman and her bark was the worst of her, but she put the fear in all of us those first days. Her crankiness came from her dislike of being the one responsible for getting this big job completed and on schedule.

In the mornings of those first weeks, we three new aspirants – Denise, Margaret, and myself - spent time with Sr. Chiarina and Sr. Olga in the main convent. Sr. Chiarina was the tailor and Sr. Olga was a woman of all work. She measured us loosely with a well-used cloth tape measure. I wondered if the measure was held so loosely around our chests and waists because our school uniforms would then be suitably baggy or if she was studiously avoiding any actual contact between her fingers and our persons.

Mother of Sorrows High School required all students to wear uniforms. It made dressing for school easier on the students and also saved parents from having to buy quantities of stylish clothes for fashion-crazy girls. Students wore a collarless, dark blue blazer, white cotton blouse, and blue-gray plaid, pleated skirt that stopped below the knee. Aspirants wore similar suits with white cotton blouses but ours were heavy serge, grey-blue in skirt and jacket. Our skirt was bulky and way below the knee, and the jacket was usually two sizes larger than necessary. Sr. Chiarina must have decided that we needed room to grow and gave us quite a bit. Our feet were in serious black leather, lace-up, low-heeled work shoes. Stockings or knee socks completed the look. Over the months, our skirts got shiny and stretched out in the back from all the sitting and studying we did. Not glamorous, but I wasn't looking for glamour.

All of us sewed on the uniforms; some sewed better than others. My grandma had taught me to sew and embroider from my fourth year, but even that was not good enough for Sr. Chiarina. Denise and Margaret and I, being new girls, had to help with our uniforms. We sewed and ripped out the poor stitches, and sewed again. After several mornings spent working on our school clothes, Mother Evarista came by the sewing room to check on the progress.

"Sr. Chiarina, how are these girls doing? With school starting in a week, I expect they are all nearly finished with their work?" Mother asked.

"Oh Madre, these American girls, they cannot put three stitches in a straight line. After two stitches, the rest start following the road to Fatima!" Sr. Chiarina moved her hand in front of her in a wavy line. "I really don't know how we are going to finish. Look at this seam, and this pocket is getting ready to fall off. This is just disgraceful. No one made them sew in their homes. Now they come here and stitch, stitch like they are working with a shovel and a hoe. How are we going to be finished in time for school?" Sr. Chiarina held her head with both hands and whirled about to stare at us. Her eyes were big and her mouth was pushed up into a shelf.

Margaret, Denise, and I sat quietly, staring back and then dropping our eyes to our work. Denise bit her lip.

"Well, Sister, my grandma showed me how to..." I began to explain, but Mother turned toward me and waved her forefinger sharply at me to stop talking. I sat with my mouth still open, but somehow I pulled the words back that I was preparing to say.

"Chiarina," Mother said, "I know you don't like to do it, but we had better get out the *macchina* and move along. When you help them with their profession clothes, then you can start well ahead and do things as you like them to be done – the right way. And you had better get Sr. Olga and Sr. Agnes to help with this. These *ragazze* need more time to learn how to be useful in God's house." She nodded confidently. "We will teach them step by step, *a poco a poco.*" With these words, Mother calmed Sr. Chiarina and as she gave us an appraising look, we also learned that our talents were going to have to be improved to stay in God's house, No slouches allowed.

I had already passed my freshman year as a regular, live-at-home student, traveling daily to Mother of Sorrows High School, so I was familiar with Mother of Sorrows High School. Classes began, as almost every school did in those days, on the Tuesday after Labor Day. First day is always full of excitment – getting the right books in the right order, finding your classroom before the bell rings, seeing what your teacher was like and how they taught. In the first week, you find out whose class is going to be breezy, whose will take effort, whose will be dead time. What I forgot to think about is the reaction of my freshman friends and classmates to the change in my attire. Last year I was wearing the blue plaid uniform with the kicky pleated skirt, and this year I stood there in the greyish bulky jacket and the wide, dumpy skirt of the aspirancy. Really, a more shapeless suit was not to be found.

Pat Heenan stopped in her tracks with her mouth open when we both walked into homeroom.

"Sally, why are you wearing that uniform?" she gasped. "What did you do? Did you go and join the convent over the summer?"

I hadn't thought out my answer to this most likely of questions, so I just nodded and headed toward a desk. Behind me, Mary Jean Pugh tapped me on the shoulder and said."Did you join the convent? Why did you do that? Don't you like boys anymore?"

I half-turned around to see her better and said, "Mary Jean, I wanted to be a sister, like Sr. Agnes is. My parents wouldn't let me come here the first year but now they did. It's okay. We will still play duets, you and me." She was my duet partner since we were both piano students of Sr. Christine. Mary Jean was the one who practiced so she got to play the lead in the classical pieces that we played, like Mendelssohn's *Scherzo*. I, being the romantic, sloppy player, got to play the lead in the lyrical things, like *Rhapsody in Blue*.

Algebra was first hour. Not bad at all. Miss Azzarello was short and curvy, and very young, but put on a tough face to keep us in line. Then Biology with the indestructible green counters and little sinks for every two students, and waxy trays for dissecting annelids and frogs. Next was Latin with skinny Mr. Hudacek. He also seemed quite young, not very handsome, and I wondered why a person his age would have chosen Latin for his major. Maybe he was a failed seminary student and now he had to earn his way in the world. Latin turned out to be the best class for me. Declensions of every noun was a toe-stubber but once I memorized the form endings, Latin fell into place like a big, ancient puzzle. And wow – these people could plan their thoughts so far ahead that they put the verb at the very end of the sentence. How do you talk like that "John, because studying of little value to you seems, into woodshed with stick striped of bark, the situation to go us requires." What a scavenger hunt it seemed.

Lunch came next in the school cafeteria. The cafeteria ladies could tell by our uniforms that we were the convent girls and did not pay for our lunches. The four of us with early lunch sat together at a table because we had already learned from Sr. Marguerite's talks that we were to be "in the world, but not of the world." Sitting with the "regular" girls brought the danger of hearing conversations about boys and dating, lipstick and clothes, even worse, pregnancy. These topics would be a terrible distraction from our work of building greater intimacy with God, so fraternizing or sororizing was to be kept to a minimum. For me, this was fine in the first weeks, since I was still rather nervous about doing something wrong and getting sent home from the convent. Later, as friendships developed with the regular girls, I wanted to listen to their chatter and hear about their lives and loves, but there was no way, at least at lunch. We could engage with them between classes without drawing any attention from the sisters. Lunches, however, were separate. So I ate quietly with Nancy, Colette, and Lois, talking about our classes or the doings at the motherhouse until one of the regular girls plugged in the jukebox.

Jukebox was allowed for the last 15 minutes of lunch but sometimes the girls started a little early, stretching dance time to 20 minutes. A double line of blue-plaid clad females would be doing the Stroll down the west side of the cafeteria, twirling and sliding their way down the long line while the Shirelles sang "Soldier Boy," and there was faster, sexier movement to Little Eva's "The Loco-Motion." Lois kept her eyes on the book she was reading and Colette watched them with a scientific interest as if categorizing them for a paper, but Nancy and I had hot, eager eyes on the dancers. We knew we weren't going to dance, but we really wanted to. My dancing was awkward, not an inborn talent, but I loved to dance. It always made me feel like a dryad or a faun in the forest, earthy and pagan. Of course, I knew this had to be given up for Jesus, subsumed into a worthy sacrifice. And I did, but I still wanted to dance. Those last fifteen minutes of lunch hour were my favorite time of the school day, except for Glee Club.

After lunch there was World History and English II. Religion with Sr. Agnes finished the schedule of work. Last hour of the day was Glee Club. A mystery to me why you called a class a club but it was the best hour of school. Young Sister Christine was about four foot ten with her shoes on. She was round of cheek, bright of eye, and always smiling, even while disciplining the altos, who were always talking when they should not. We began our Christmas music in Early October since the forty minute class went by quickly what with stopping for intercom announcements from the main office, taking attendance, getting your own music folder, asking for the song sheet that you can't find because you were late last class, milling around to your correct place on the risers, listening to the altos go over their part several times, and finally singing the songs ensemble and properly. Sr. Christine would sometimes play parts for rehearsal but Mary Jean Pugh was the accompanist for the Glee Club. She was the same girl I played duets with

Jackie Neath sang next to me in the Soprano section. Jackie was a beautiful girl with big, bouffant, teased black hair. She was taking independent study French because she spoke French fluently from her home life. Jackie was totally chic in my eyes. Also very kind. When we started working on a song with the words Joyeux Noel in it, she worked on our pronunciation. All the sopranos near her were taught to say "zwah- yehhrrr" Noel where you have to kind of swallow the r's but let them be heard. I felt a little of her chic-ness rub off on me – wishful thinking.

By Thanksgiving, we new aspirants had pretty much settled down into the convent routine and pretty much knew what was expected and also what the consequences were if we fell short of expectations. I learned that Mother Evarista's smile was more a public thing than an inner state. When guests were present, she deigned to visit with them and nod and smile, but her black brows were usually pressed far down and she was hard to read. She was short and compact and I sensed a physical strength and purpose in her that was not used. Her gaze was often upon us young ones. I could feel her calculating whether each of us was fervent enough, serious enough, humble and obedient enough, hard-working enough. Most of the time I tried to avoid her gaze since there was no good response that I could think of. "Good morning, Mother," or "Good evening, Mother," were the only responses I could think of. Engaging in an actual conversation was unthinkable.

Mother Evarista made every decision that needed to be made in running a convent of some twenty nuns, a high school with over four hundred young women students, a boarding school of eighty children, and a convent training school of the six of us. Her lieutenants in this endeavor were Sr. Felicita, high school principal, Sr. Raphael, grade school commandant, and Sr. Marguerite, aspirancy mistress. I didn't think about it at the time, but presumably Sr. Felicita had some background in education administration. The high school was accredited with the State of Illinois, and there were no doubt many requirements that Sr. Felicita had to meet. As for Raphael, she was just good with kids, especially boys.

The boarders had classes but I hardly ever saw them, day or night. They were kept in the north side of the building and the sisters and aspirants only used to south wing, and then only for the kitchen and refectory, and the business office upstairs and the parlor for visitors. Raphael kept the boarders busy with homework and sports. There was a basketball court laid out in composition vinyl tile in the basement of the boarding school and many days you could hear the hollow *thonk* of an under-inflated basketball being passed around.

While she watched over her charges, Raphael made rosaries out of decayed roses. She got roses from the funeral parlors in town on a regular basis since they all knew what she wanted with them. She chopped them up and allowed them to ferment in big tubs. When a new batch was brewing, the air was redolent of alcohol and dead flowers. After they became a big, soggy mess, she would add some secret ingredients and stir. Another week or so went by before she started making beads. She used a tiny round spoon, like a miniature melon baller, to pull off a piece of rose mixture about the size of chewed wad of gum. Rolling this between her black-stained fingers, she made a well-rounded bead and set it in another tray to dry. When a day had passed and the bead was half-dry, she pierced each one with a large needle to make a hole for the wire. A few days after that, she started wiring the beads into decades for ten Hail Marys, interrupted by a larger bead, or perhaps a real glass bead for the Our Father. Five decades were wired together with a medal of the Blessed Virgin for a centerpiece. Then three more Hail Mary beads, followed by the Glory Be to the Father beads were wired down from the medal, capped off with a small silver crucifix from the jewelry findings store. You say the Apostles' Creed at the crucifix to start the rosary, but it is the last thing put on when you make a rosary. Sr. Raphael had a great following of old Catholics who would bring her the roses from their loved ones' funerals, and she would make them rosaries for remembrance. Maybe she got ten dollars for a rosary, maybe twenty-five. Some people took them to Rome and had them blessed by the Pope. That made Raphael so proud of her messy work.

Colette used to spend time down on the basketball court with Sr. Raphael, helping her mind the evil-smelling mixture that became a rosary. Colette, a natural rebel, liked Sr. Raphael's devil-may-care attitude. When the boys were noisy or disobedient, Raphael loudly called them out, shouted them down, and sent them upstairs to their rooms to wait for further discussion of their particular offense.

Colette herself got into trouble when Sr. Antoinette took a shortcut through the boys' playroom to the kitchen. Antoinette moved like a tall sailing ship. Her straight back and head thrown up high caused her white cook's veil to blow backward like a canvas sail. She threw open the door, glided through the knot of six-twelve year old kids, and turned her head and entire upper body to greet Sr. Raphael. When she saw Colette standing next to Raphael at the rose-fermenting table, stirring the mess with a big steel spoon, Antoinette jerked her head up even higher. She stopped and stared, batting her eyes and raising her nearly-white eyebrows.

"Sister, why is this aspirant down here in the boys' room and not over in the aspirancy house with the rest of her group?" Antoinette had righteousness down to a science. Her feet were planted; her palms were spread wide, open to receive an answer to her query. Her eye was fixed on the cringing aspirant with blackened fingertips.

Raphael was calm and not at all distressed. She was ready to guard her territory. "Antoinette, I have eleven young men to take care of and make sure they have their homework finished, and make sure they get enough exercise so they don't start walloping on each other. And besides that, there were three funerals last week, and all of them want to have rosaries made for their families, and they want them ASAP. Now, this girl is very helpful to me. She pays attention to my instructions and treats the rose mixture with respect and care. That gives me more time to attend to the boys. Don't you think I should have a little help here?"

Raphael half -turned to three boys who were fighting over a toy tank. "James, that tank belongs to Charlie. Give it back and ask him nicely if you can play with it for a while. Charlie, can't you share that for a few minutes? James is not going to take it out of this room. And Jerome, go wipe your nose. You're dripping. Not with your hand – get a tissue," she corrected and molded the boys with a calm voice and a steady, all-seeing eye. She turned her attention back to Antoinette.

36

"Now, Antoinette, just be sweet and go get started on dinner. There is a rumor you are making your famous pesto tortellini for supper tonight. Is it true? I love your pesto."

"Sister Raphael, you know we are not to be concerned about what we eat and what we have to wear. We are simply to follow our beloved as obedient brides of Christ." Antoinette replied stiffly, but her mouth turned up a little at the edges. She seldom got compliments on her cooking, even though she put her whole heart and attention into it. Nuns, indeed, were not to spend time and attention on the needs of the body so no matter how she labored over a dish, no one said 'well done'. Now she straightened her back and nodded to Raphael and Collette, and sailed on down the room to the door leading to the kitchen.

"Colette, you'd better wash up and get back to your studies," Sister Raphael said with a sigh. "Antoinette won't forget this and soon she will have Mother Evarista down here to talk to me."

Colette collected her school books and headed back to the aspirancy house, avoiding the route through the kitchen.

CHAPTER 5

—— ❧ ——

Making Our Own Drama

BACK AT THE aspirancy house, we were all gathered around the dining room table, doing our homework. Each had her assigned place and the books and notebooks and dictionaries and pencil and pens filled the table to capacity. Colette and I shared most of the same classes, and Nancy also had several with us. Lois was enrolled in other classes and, of course, Margaret and Denise were freshmen and they also shared a few classes. Sr. Marguerite presided over the study table at first, but as the weeks of school went by, she often stayed upstairs in her room and corrected papers. She taught several sections of maths at the high school and had considerable homework of her own. We were a distraction to her with our whispering and jiggling and flapping of papers.

Studying was always a mystery to me so I was always finished before most of the group. I spent the remainder of the time practicing on the ancient baby grand in the parlor. This elderly instrument had been painted a brownish-green with many bouquets and angels in its various panels. Much more decorative than useful, it was working way past its viable lifespan but some dear Catholic lady had donated it to the sisters and it ended up in the aspirancy parlor. Two rooms away from the dining room, the sound of practicing still was loud and clear. Having five sets of ears listening at all times made me very uncomfortable but Sr. Marguerite insisted that I practice for my lesson. Plinking my way through Mendelssohn's Scherzo was embarrassing to me and painful for my sisters. I learned to practice the difficult things in one of the practice rooms at the high school and just play things I was already good at in the house.

Happy to get away from the table, often I would sprawl on the sofa and read my lit class assignments. *Julius Caesar* was the play for sophomore year, and Denise would sometimes grab a copy and come over to dramatize the best parts with me and Colette and Nancy. She was Julius because she was the most emotive. I took Brutus' part; he interested me in the way he changed from friend to assassin. Nancy always took the feminine readings, Calpurnia in this case. A small part but she loved it, sidling up to Caesar and clutching her blue-gray jacket by the lapels, crying

"Do not go forth to-day: call it my fear

That keeps you in the house, and not your own…. Let me, upon my knee, prevail in this."

As she knelt, clasping Denise's knees with both arms, Denise reached down and put her palm on Nancy's head. Just then Sr. Marguerite happened to walk by with a stack of geometry tests in her arms. She gave us a horrified look and dropped her papers in the nearest chair.

"Girls, what on earth are you doing?" Sister's veil belled out from her quick turn.

"Take your hands off her legs," she ordered Nancy.

Nancy quickly let go of Denise and stood up and we all stared at Sister like a clutch of rabbits. We knew we had transgressed but were not sure what the transgression was. Were we making too much noise? Was studying together wrong?

"What are you girls thinking? You do not touch each other. You know that. Have you ever seen the sisters grabbing each other about the knees? No, you have not. We keep ourselves to ourselves and do not put our hands upon another sister. Ever!" Sister turned her eyes upon each of our faces to make sure we got the point.

"But, Sister, "I ventured, "We aren't nuns yet. We're just aspirants. Those rules don't apply to us, do they?"

She became quite red in the face, and her black eyes pierced me. "Miss Jardine, if that is your present attitude, you will definitely

NOT find yourself becoming a candidate for joining this convent, or any convent. The life you are seeking here is based on our vows of Poverty, Chastity and Obedience. And you seem to be severely lacking in at least two of those virtues. You had better run off to chapel right now and spend some time on your knees thinking about how you expect to proceed in your journey toward becoming a Bride of Christ. He is not accepting unchaste and disobedient spouses right now, as far as I know." With that, she whirled about, picked up her papers, and went upstairs to her private room.

Denise and Nancy slipped back into the dining room and sat down to study. I got my coat from the entry hall and slouched away to chapel.

Several months passed before I began to understand just what the convent expected of me. Aspirants were not really part of the Order, we were more like a weedy garden that the nuns were training up to become sturdy and viable parts of their community. They were not afraid to pluck off any bad habits that showed up in our characters. Independent thinking was suddenly not a value to be pursued. Nor was wasting time in idle chatter or visiting with non-convent friends. Library time was not to include paging through LIFE and LOOK magazine and commenting on the new styles of hair and clothing. When Sr. Phillip noticed me reading anything I could find about the new Hippie trend, she told Sr. Marguerite about this and when I came to the library next time to look up current affairs, Sr. Phillip sidled past the library table where I sat and pointedly gazed over my shoulder to check up on which magazine I was reading. If it was TIME or U.S. News & World Report, she moved along. If it was Newsweek or LOOK or LIFE, she stayed close and let me know that I was under surveillance.

CHAPTER 6

Home for Christmas

SOON THE YEAR wound down to December and it was time for us to go home for Christmas. Mama and Papa came to pick me up after the last class. They parked and came into the aspirant house to help me with my things and to greet Sr. Marguerite. Sister was smiling and friendly to everyone that day. Her charges were leaving her for three weeks; she was officially out of work until the start of school in January. My parents brought her a large tray of battered shrimp and cocktail sauce from the restaurant they owned in Tinley Park for the sisters' dinner table. Also an extra-large fruitcake. Smiles for the shrimp, polite thanks for the fruitcake. And I picked up my small Samsonite and headed off to the car.

Looking forward to going home for months, the actual visit turned out to be oddly out of focus for me, maybe for my family, too. Three months of convent training had started to take effect. I found it strange to embrace grandparents, cousins, aunts and uncles. Touching a body was strange and I half-expected to be reprimand. When Grandma Swanson gave me a welcoming hug, my arms stayed limply by my sides and my cheek turned for her kiss. None returned. Having a television turned on for much of the day was a noisy intrusion. And the omnipresence of food and beverages gave a bacchanalian glow to the days. Visiting relatives brought plates of Italian rosette cookies and bottles of wine, brandy, and anisette. Mama and Papa prepared a Christmas Eve buffet for grandparents, aunts, uncles, cousins, friends who lived nearby. Always a ham with a diamond pattern cut into its fat, studded with whole cloves and maraschino cherries, a platter of golden deviled eggs dusted with paprika, celery sticks with Kaukauna cheese out the brown crocks with lids that were fastened shut by a wire device stuffed up the middle, fried chicken from the restaurant, a huge tray of ribs with a half-gallon of barbeque sauce, a wooden bucket of pickled herring, and trays of cakes and cookies, and fruitcakes made shiny from being bathed in brandy or rum. Sweets were not my mom's forte but plenty of goodies came with the visiting relatives. And she bustled around in her Christmas corsage of red and white chrysanthemums, greeting everyone, tossing their coats to me to put upstairs on her bed.

"Why aren't you eating this good ham?" my cousin Bobby Lou asked me. She was trying on the jacket of the Black Watch plaid Pendleton jacket that Grandma Jardine had given her. Bobbi Lou, her older sister Wavelyn, and I, being the only granddaughters at this point, got identical wool suits. It was much easier for Grandma to give all the girls that same thing.

"I'm going to Midnight Mass at St. George's," I answered, knowing she wouldn't understand, Protestant that she was. I pulled my new jacket out of the wrapping papers and tried it on, too.

"Well, eat before you go," she suggested. She pulled the plaid skirt from her Christmas box and shook out the pleats, smiling and holding it at her waist. Her shiny brown curls bounced as she twisted from side to side. I liked mine, too, but I worried that it might be too short for the convent.

"No, Bobby Lou. I have to fast before Holy Communion." Snugly said.

"Well, that's a dopey way to spend Christmas Eve," Bobby Lou said. "How are you going to have any fun when you are fasting? Can't you even have eggnog?"

"Nothing. Absolutely nothing." I folded up the coat and put it back into the box, delighting in my staunch piety.

Mama drove Grandma Anna and me to church. The air was so cold you almost couldn't take a breath. The night sky was black, with no stars. Only the light from the street lights glowed on snowy lawns and made sparkles of the airborne snow. Papa stayed at the house with the rest of the party. He was a convert and not as devout as the rest of us and also, someone needed to play host. My Italian grandmother was pleased to have some company at Midnight Mass. Other years when she invited me to come with her, I refused to give up the party. Now I felt no choice was open to me but to attend. The nuns from St. George's School would be looking for me, and for Nancy and Colette.

And later, in the candlelit shadows of St. George's, I felt the calm slip over me. What I missed at home in my mother's house came to me in the silent wait for the midnight hour. A cough sounded here and there in the chilly air in the church. Overcoats gave off the scent of cold and snow, overpowered by the scent of the altar greenery. The organ playing a classical prelude, and the white and gold vestments only used for Christmas pulled me into an alternate space. Altar boys in red chasubles covered by white lacey surplices carried thick candles in procession up the main aisle of the church. The organ played "Angels We Have Heard on High" and the congregation stood up as Father O'Connell walked in behind the altar boys carrying the linen-wrapped stature of the baby Jesus that would be placed in the empty manger later in the service. Father O'Connell carried the big red Missal; this night it was covered with a white and gold strip of cloth. When they reached the transept, the boys filed to both sides and Father mounted the steps to the altar with his heavy burden. He set the Book up on its heavy wood stand and moved to the back of the altar. Genuflecting slowly and kissing the altar relic, he undid the heavy clasp on his outer cloak and handed it to one of the boys who took it away to the sacristy. Father still wore the embroidered festival chasuble. He moved back down the three stairs and turned his back to the congregation. He gestured for one of the boys to bring the Missal forward. The youngest altar boy carried the heavy book to Father, who pushed him back and over to the right a little by his shoulders, and then Father intoned the Latin words to begin the Mass, ""Introibo ad altare Dei," (I will go up to the altar of God) and the altar boys answered together in their practiced rhythm, "Ad Deum qui lætificat iuventutem meam" (to the God who gives joy to my youth).

After the Christmas break, the aspirants returned to Mother of Sorrows. I detected some of the same feeling of relief among the others as I felt in my own heart. Structured by the bells, our lives resumed quietly, flowing inexorably toward the goal of becoming a Bride of Christ. We were beginning to need the quiet and the calm.

CHAPTER 7

John Kennedy and The Beatles

BY MY JUNIOR year, 1963-64, the world outside had changed on multiple fronts. Clothes were becoming wilder and shorter. Not ours, of course, but the high school girls came to orientation in crazy flower-covered, psychedelic-print short dresses. Their hair was long and parted in the middle, swaying like drapes over their shoulders. Some wore chunky shoes with platform heels that made them seem two or three inches taller, but Sr. Philip made them take those off when they came into the library. She would not have all that clunking around when people were trying to read.

Our convent life underwent a change that I didn't expect. Sister Marguerite was replaced as our Aspirant Mistress by Sister Emilia. Sister Emilia was pure Italian, about forty-five years old, with swarthy checks and dark eyebrows that expressed her inner thoughts precisely. She spoke English very well and was very congenial with our parents but we soon learned that she intended to re-shape the Aspirancy into a firmer, more European model. And she created a baroque, Italianate power structure over us that was alien to our American laissez faire mindset.

Since many things we did needed permission, we had to ask Sister Emilia if we could talk to her, and to wait with fluttery stomachs until the appointed time. Sitting in the dining room, doing our homework, we would be called upstairs one by one for counseling. As I was a girl who still needed affirmation from an adult, I sat with a mix of anxiety and jealousy as others got to meet with Sister Emilia and I had to wait my turn. Wanting to be the favorite,

I made up situations that needed permission: "Sister Emilia, may I join the Library Club? I know Sister Phillip needs more help with restocking the books." "Sister Emilia, may I stay after school and practice with Mary Jean Pugh? We have a recital next month and the Mendelssohn piece is not going well." "Sister Emilia, may I call my mother and invite her to the awards ceremony?" Anything I could think of to get a few minutes of her attention, I used with no remorse. I was especially jealous of Kathy. She seemed to have the longest talks with Sister and most often. Colette, on the other hand, eschewed the whole process. Her style was to do what she needed, and keep her head down, hoping to slide under the Italian radar.

Sister Emilia called me in to her room one evening for counseling. I entered and knelt down before her chair, as we were taught. She told me to stand up and turn around. I did that, wondering of my skirt was ripped or too short. After a full revolution, she said, "Sit down. Some of the sisters are worried that you are losing too much weight."

Surprised that my loss of baby fat was a cause for concern, I said, "Well, Sister, I eat lots of food at mealtime, but we don't do all the snacking here in the convent that I used to do at home, so it's not surprising that I lost some weight. And we do lots more physical work than I did at home. I was always too plump anyway. Mama used to scold me for eating candy bars and hiding the wrappers under my mattress."

"Even so, Mother Evarista wants me to make sure you don't get too thin. If you are too thin and get sick, you have nothing left to lose."

She took me downstairs to the basement and got out a clean glass and spoon, took an egg and some milk out of the refrigerator and set them on the table. Folding back her black sleeves, she started to demonstrate the technique. "This is what she wants you to do," she said, "every day after school, before you do anything else, come down to the basement refrigerator and take out an egg" – shudders here from me as an egg was my least favorite thing to consume – "and beat it with a tablespoon of sugar and a little dollop of milk until it is very light and fluffy. Then put in a half cup of Moscato and drink it down. It will give you extra strength. We used to do this during the war whenever we could get some eggs and some sugar."

"Thank you, Sister. I will start tomorrow," I said.

"You will start right now," she said, and handed me the Moscato egg cream that she had just made. I gulped it down with trepidation. Not bad; I could get to like this kind of egg.

Junior year my schedule included Miss Azzarello for French and Miss Blanca Gonzalez for Spanish and Miss O'Brien for American History, Sister Christine for Glee Club and Piano, Sister Agnes for homeroom and Religion. One Thursday in November, the History class was having a discussion about the presidency of Andrew Jackson and his treatment of Native Americans. At 11 am, the intercom clicked into life and, in a wobbly voice, Mrs. LaRotonda made an announcement that President Kennedy had been shot and was being taken to a hospital in Dallas. Shrieks of surprise and disbelief rose from many of the girls. Some started up out of their desks and rushed to hug someone, clinging to the known in what seemed a surreal moment. Miss O'Brien walked quickly from her desk to the classroom door. With her hand on the doorknob, she turned back and looked right at me.

"Miss Jardine, start the rosary. We need to pray now. I'll go see what is going on. Perhaps this is a mistake by the news channels." She closed the door with a snap.

My head was whirling with thoughts of our handsome president and his chic wife, all the pretty pictures I had been mooning over in LIFE Magazine when Sr. Philip was busy elsewhere in the library. Jackie in her French gowns, little John-John under his daddy's desk, Caroline riding a pony. How could someone want to shoot them?

How could God let this happen here – here in America? Unfair. Crazy to think the FBI and all the police surrounding the President could let this happen. I pulled the rosary out of my baggy skirt pocket and began, "I believe in God, the Father Almighty..." Several voices joined in but some girls were still sobbing in each other's arms.

That night something unprecedented happened in the convent. After prayers, we sat down to supper and there was a television in the refectory. Instead of a sister reading to us while we ate, we watched Walter Cronkite reporting on the death of the president. We watched over and over as the shiny black cars wound through the Dallas neighborhood, our eyes were glued to him. The gleam of sunshine on his big Kennedy family hair, Jackie's bobbing pink pill box hat. Thinking about how we girls all wanted pillbox hats for Easter. Suddenly he was down and men in suits were running in all directions like ants. The older Italian sisters buzzed with questions since they didn't understand the commentary very clearly. Walter Cronkite kept removing his glasses and putting them back on, choking up and trying to remain professional as he told us perhaps the most important story of the decade.

Sister Addolorata's supper, hastily prepared, was mostly ignored by all of us. She and Sister Antoinette came in from the kitchen and watched the news with all of us. Sister Antoinette made loud exclamations of shock and disbelief. With a whoosh of starched veil, Sister Ernesta turned her head toward the back of the refectory and shushed Antoinette. Ernesta was having trouble understanding the rapid English reporting. The news hit the sisters very hard. This President was their darling in a special way: he was Catholic and finally they had a president they could feel connected with in a spiritual way. His loss would be more than a political loss to them. It would be a loss of the heart.

After it became clear there was no more hope and no more news, Mother Evarista told us all to clear up the dishes and come to the chapel. There, with thick knots in our throats, we began the

Miserere psalm, "Have mercy on me, O God, according to your great goodness.

Fall semester wound down to Christmas and the break. After we returned to school for the spring semester, girls appeared in clothes that were becoming wilder and shorter. On our semester breaks and our summer home time, I had eagerly followed the rise of the hippie culture. Like any "normal" teenaged girl, I listened to the radio whenever possible. If we were traveling somewhere with one of the younger nuns, they might turn on the radio, but not for long. We only got snippets of songs, but loved them anyway. Janis Joplin, Jimi Hendrix, Sonny and Cher, Roy Orbison, the Beach Boys. I really loved the pictures in LIFE magazine showing girls and boys in long hair, parted in the middle, wearing beads and long vests and flowing blouses. They looked somewhat medieval and very gentle. The gentle part of the culture appealed to me so much, and somehow I felt a kinship with them and their flashing peace signs, fingers lifted up in a V for peace and love. In my chosen profession I would be caring for other people, as the hippies obviously cared for each other. Their joyful dancing in the streets, skirts whirling, gave me hope that someday soon there would be peace for the world.

On a chilly February day in 1964, several girls came running into the glee classroom, talking all at once. Squealing, and hugging each other, they told Sister and the rest of the class about the Ed Sullivan show they saw last night. A new band called The Beatles sang and each of the girls had their favorite band member. Next day, one of the girls brought a 45 RPM and Sister Christine – always indulgent to her students – allowed her to play it on the classroom record player. A relentless drumbeat began and soon a British-accented voice began to sing, *"O yeah, I'll tell you something, I think you'll understand."* Every face had a big smile. Something about this band was just so cool, and we all wanted to be cool. When the flip side was played, John Lennon sang, *"That boy took my love away;*

he'll regret it someday. But this boy wants you back again." Oh, my knees just gave way. I had to sit down. Nearly letting out a squeal myself, I turned my face to look at Colette. She had a grim and serious look that warned me, "That's not for us." So I swallowed my screech and settled down quietly in my seat, but watching with great interest all that the girls were sharing.

Sr. Christine let the outside girls bring in their records, mostly on Fridays when she was tired of teaching. Some would dance in the aisles between desks. Convent life did not include this type of music but I listened hard to the conversations. I learned the words to *Pretty Woman* and *You Don't Own Me.* That one I sang along with the record but my eyes were on Colette. When they played *Dancing in the Street,* the girls gyrated in the aisles between the desks. I did a little chair dancing but I knew it looked ridiculous. Me in my baggy, steel blue uniform, bobbing and smiling to the happy beat. Sister Emilia would have something to say if she came to the music wing and saw me, so I snuffed out the joy of the back beat and the singing that so easily fired me up.

All this racket was only possible because the people who built our high school wisely placed the music classes in a wing far away from the more sedate classes like history and lit. The only thing close to us was the gym, and that was often empty.

CHAPTER 8

Denise Challenges the Rules

DENISE CAME HOME from school one April afternoon with special news. She was going to run for Senior Class President. This was baffling to me. I didn't think the nuns would let her do that. We were always taught to keep out of the spotlight, to do our work and come back to the convent to do the work of preparing to be spouses of Christ. And Denise was wanting to be the leader of the Junior class!

Of course, this was just like her. Denise was a natural leader. Every time we got into trouble about overstepping the rules, Denise was at the heart of the incident. She was the one who got us started singing little Operettas in Sr. Marguerite's classroom. After we finished our homework there, we usually had some time before chapel and Denise would start up with an improvised aria from some popular Broadway show – "Westside Story" was our favorite, but we also did "My Fair Lady" and "The Sound of Music." That was one we could really relate to. We all saw ourselves as the resistant Maria. The rest of us would join her one by one, some singing harmony. Soon we were dancing around and playing the parts, but not too loud because we knew this would get frowned upon at the very least.

There wasn't much in the way of campaigning, and Denise did win quite easily. She came back to the aspirancy very excited that day. Sister Emilia asked what was going on. And Margaret said, "Denise won the election, Sister. She will be the Senior Class President!"

Sister Emilia gave us all that Italian disapproving look and asked, "What does a Senior Class President have to do?"

Nancy said it was a great honor and it shows that her classmates see Denise as a good leader. She will have to run class meetings and hold debates about senior class decisions. They have to decide on their motto and their class colors, and when to hold the prom and what the theme of the prom should be.

"The Senior Prom!" Sr. Emilia said, "We in religion do not go to proms. I will have to talk to Mother Superior about this. You girls cannot just go around accepting offices and honors without her permission."

She left the study room right then and walked over to the motherhouse to consult. We hadn't realized that this idea would be foreign to Sister Emilia. She was educated in Italy and we had no idea what kind of high school experience she might have had, but it was sure to be quite different from our American high school, even though ours was a girls' high school.

"Denise, what if they say you cannot be the class president? I asked her quietly. "Will you bow out and let Cheri take the office?"

Denise looked grim. "I don't know," she said. "I didn't think this would be such a big deal."

"We should have known," said Nancy. "They never want us to do public things unless it is something they think up."

Later Sr. Emilia came back from the motherhouse looking somewhat mollified.

"Mother Evarista and I talked about this Senior Class President issue and she decided it could be a good thing for the convent. Denise's example of how a young Catholic woman should conduct herself will do much to lead her classmates in Christian living," she said. "Denise can use the opportunity to perhaps bring other girls to recognize their vocation in Christ. She may keep the position that her classmates elected her to," Sister Emilia said. She appeared to have accepted the situation wholeheartedly since it might result in a couple more aspirants or postulants.

CHAPTER 9

Heading Toward a Decision

SENIOR YEAR BEGAN for me and Nancy and Colette with no particular physical change but an attitude change was occurring, at least in myself. I was beginning to look at the idea of college and what the plan should be for the rest of my life. Foremost was the question – would the Servite order accept me as a postulant next August? And the second question was – did I really want to commit myself to this life? Some of the aspirants, everyone but me I thought, prayed with such fervor and willingness while I usually felt like I was only waiting for the services to get over so we could get out of chapel and do something else. Meditation made me fall asleep and saying the rosary was an unwelcome discipline. I could imagine God himself falling asleep listening to us nuns chanting the same prayer over and over and over to the heavens: "Ave Maria, gratia plena, Dominus tecum. Benedicta tu in mulieribus". When I guardedly glanced at Nancy and Colette, they appeared to be wrapped up in the meditations on the mysteries of the rosary. Their heads were bowed and their eyes were closed as they contemplated the moments in the life of Jesus. So, what was wrong with me? Was I not made of the right stuff to be a nun? Why couldn't I enjoy praying like everybody else? When would the ecstasy of Saint Theresa be mine? I tamped down these thoughts and tried to keep the appearance of piety. To question right now would mean that I would have to take a stand one way or the other, and I was not ready for that.

Senior year also brought new classes: Journalism with Mrs. Brennan. She was a short, grey-haired lady with a bowl haircut, but there was nothing grandmotherly about her. Always on the move, she delegated stories and assignments to us like a magician setting out cards. We only had one camera so our faculty interviews and coverage of the intramural volleyball games often had no photo attached. Of course, when we sought quotes from the principal, Sister Felicita, the camera person had to be there. Mrs. Brennan also taught creative writing during the journalism course. We produced and printed up a little magazine called "Whispers and Shouts," filled with our creative efforts. Finally, I am published! The cover of the little tome was yellow and black, very jazzy we thought, with the hand-drawn title in white. So impressive at the time. This was heady stuff. I purchased several copies so Mama and Papa could have one, and Grandma Anna, and myself. Somewhere in my photo and old letters box, the little booklet is lying, collecting dust.

I was signed up for Chemistry class with Miss Calderero. She was a tiny, dark-haired young woman. Probably this was her first year teaching after getting her degree. She bustled about the science lab, showing us how to titrate and set up experiments to identify compounds. The math of it was fascinating. Chemistry showed how you never lose anything, not a single atom is lost. It is just recombining to become something else. Quite a life lesson. Besides her cool outfits, the most delightful thing about Miss Calderero was her inability to say "specific gravity." A chemistry teacher has to say that phrase hundreds of times in Chemistry 101, and every single time she said "pacific gravity." I still smile about it.

Graduation sped toward us, causing the usual flutter about ceremonies and speeches. Our school graded us in a percentage scale, not an alphabetical scale, and every year, I ended up in competition with Peggy Lavin for first place. Of course, I feigned indifference, but I was very interested to see which of us would be Valedictorian and which would be Salutatorian. The whole world would know your standing when they read the program.

On the final days of classes, we got our grades from each teacher. My allies, mostly Colette and Nancy, did lightning fast calculating to see which of us was ahead. After all the grades were in, I beat Peggy Lavin by a couple hundredths of a point, we were that close. Modestly rejoicing, I started to think what I would possibly have to say in my valedictory speech. A few days later, the programs for graduation night were printed and Colette, Nancy and I went up to the office to look at them. I couldn't believe it. Kathy Des Forges, class president, was delivering the speech I was supposed to have earned. This was a total change of tradition and common usage and I knew exactly why it had happened. In the convent, you never put yourself forward and you never make a personal splash. The nuns did this so I would be humbled. And I was not. I was furious. And this fury, too, had to be hidden or I would have to confess it to the Aspirant Mistress as a fault. So I put on an indifferent face. In any case, there would be no recourse; I knew that. At least my friends knew that I had earned that honor, and Colette was all for confronting Mother Evarista. I said no; it would make no difference. This was their way of keeping us away from the secular glories. It was probably for the best.

Now our last summer vacation was sneaking toward us and all the aspirants were tasked to clean the entire aspirancy house and pack all their things back into the trunk that they brought with them. Somehow, a person's possessions always increase, even if that person is a person in religion. Squeezing everything back into the truck took planning. There were spiritual reading books given to us by Mother Superior and Sister Emilia so we would stay close to our religion during the summer and not get carried away by secular friends. There were notebooks and school prizes and mementos from classmates.

And holy cards, dozens of them. Nuns gift each other with holy cards at the slightest provocation. A birthday will bring a dozen

cards with Bible verses and inspiring pictures of saints being cruci-
fied upside down or roasted over hot coals by their tormentors. St.
Lawrence actually is attributed to have said "Turn me over: I am
done on this side." The more modern holy cards were desirable.
They usually were a verse or motto done up in lovely calligraphy
with a small pen drawing of a dove or a flame. These were highly
prized and given between special friends. Some of us collected
sayings in a little notebook and then would sit down and create
holy cards with layers of colored tissue and fancy lettering, and give
them to each other for inspiration.

The cards encouraged solidarity among us young Americans as
we often did not know what the Italian hierarchy wanted from us.
The superiors seemed to want a mixture of submission and obedience combined with a demonstration of willingness to serve God
in any way that they saw fit. As we aspirants gained confidence
and maturity during our four years of high school studies, we often
ran into trouble interpreting Sister Emilia's directives. She would
tell us to clean the chapel, and we would cheerfully start, but when
she came around to check up on our progress, she often found us
finished and lounging around on the benches, singing songs from
Camelot or, worse yet, the Top 40 song list. American clean never
stacked up to Old World Italian clean. If I dusted the fronts and tops
of the library of liturgy books, I was wrong. I should have taken them
all out of the bookcase and dusted over and under and around
and on top of them and set them all back in dustless splendor. If
Nancy and Colette had dust mopped the terrazzo floor, they were
wrong. They should have swept and then got water and brushes
and scrubbed the floor. And dusting the pews, of course, was just
wasted effort. We had to get the bucket and rags and Murphy's Oil
Soap and wash and dry every inch of the fifty or so pews in chapel.
Not just twice a year but every week. This work ethic really made
me long for summer vacation.

CHAPTER 10

Last Summer

IMPOSSIBLE AS IT seemed, we finally cleaned everything in the Aspirant House and chapel and refectory and boarding school to the satisfaction of Sister Emilia, and were able to call our parents to come take us home for the summer. Mama and Papa came to pick up me and my trunk. My clothes and shoes were packed, my school uniform was left hanging in the closet. Someone, probably Sister Floriana, would clean it and press it in preparation for another aspirant in the fall. We sped south toward Tinley Park and, to my convent-molded eyes, the houses and stores and roads were achingly familiar and strange at the same time. Three months of carefree freedom would be overshadowed by the need to make a decision.

Before we went home, Papa stopped at the restaurant to check up on some things. Mama and I got out and went into the kitchen. I got smiles and greetings from Marian, Gert and Flo and many of the cooks and waitresses. Most cooks and waitresses stayed at Jardine's for years and so they knew me from my early years. I never worked at the restaurant except in the summers when Papa had me do payroll, but I did this at home. Busboys also came over and said hello. Tommy Bockstahler was there from my grade school class, and Artie Neff from the year behind him. Marie Sorenson's gorgeous Italian son, Billy, smiled and glided by with a bin full of dirty dishes. "Are you still in that convent, Sally Sue?" he grinned. He knew I was. And Tommy asked, "Are you gonna stay home now or are you going back there? He, like most boys, was baffled by a girl's decision to be a nun. I think boys take this as a personal affront that a girl would choose celibacy over them. I answered all questions seriously, never being the type of girl to whom flirting comes easily. But I was pleased by their attention, even though I didn't know what to do with it.

At home, I lived a lazy life, incredibly lazy by comparison with my convent life. My folks knew it was only for three months so they didn't push me to get a job. Grandma Anna and I took care of the house, American style, not convent style. I took a course of piano at the Sherwood School of Music in downtown Chicago, arranged by Sister Christine. The teacher that year was an Argentine gentleman with a very small sense of humor. Senor Something. He told me I had been playing pieces beyond my capacity and then gave me a very difficult Papillion piece to work on. I had absolutely no motivation to work with him so that part of the course was not useful. The theory classes always grabbed my interest because I was a math person. This was my third summer at Sherwood. I don't know what my parents had to pay for tuition but they were happy to do it. Mom and Dad always fostered my music and my reading. Good parents. But Dad would sometimes grab my book and say, "Get outside and play or something. Take the dog for a walk." He didn't understand the lure of the 19th Century British novel to a young girl.

During that summer after my senior year, Mama hatched the idea of me having a reunion party for my eighth grade class, and I was happy to plan with her. All of the fifty-five graduates of the previous year were invited. About thirty-five showed up. Our home was right next to the forest preserve that surrounds the Chicagoland area. We had a big yard and a sizable house. Mama brought home fried chicken and ribs and potato salad from the restaurant. I gathered potato chips and pretzels and other things that kids like. Papa set up the coolers with ice and soda pop. The evening was cool enough to enjoy the fire in the outdoor fireplace. Some of my friends were the same as I remembered; others had changed, had made new alliances in their various schools. Janice and Jack were no longer an item. Steve and Barb still talked to each other but not with the locked gaze they used to have. Rusty and Joanne still had lots to say to each other although she went to a girl's school and he did not.

I tuned the radio to WLS so we could listen to the good songs and kids danced together on the patio. The boys were still doing the Twist and the Stroll, the girls had moved on to more current dances, but when the slow songs came on the radio, fewer couples formed. Maybe they just wanted to talk. We seemed to recognize the distance that four years had put between us.

In August, Aunt Esther and Uncle Phil came for their annual visit. They lived in Chicago in a brownstone and we only saw them once or twice a year. How funny. Chicago was thirty-five miles away but they could have lived in Alaska and the visiting would be the same. They were my great-aunt and –uncle and really came to see Grandma Anna more than Mom and Dad and me. Uncle Phil was grandma's favorite brother and she was always a little judgmental about Aunt Esther. Esther was Polish, which is one cause for Grandma's suspicion, but Grandma would not like anyone who had married her brother Philly.

Aunt Esther wanted to know if I was still going to be a nun.

"Of course I am," I said. "I go into the convent on August 23rd. It is the special feast day for the Mantellates and they always receive new members on that day."

"Well, I would never let one of my girls waste her life in a convent. Pearl, what are you thinking, letting a little kid go be a nun? They never have husbands. And you won't get to see her but once a year. She can pray and be a good person in her own home. This is just weird." Esther was baffled and repelled by the whole idea.

"Aunt Esther, she will be safe there. And she is just at the beginning of the nun journey. She has five years to decide if she really wants to stay there. Perpetual vows are only after five years of trying it out. Sally has wanted to do this since she was twelve, so I think we should let her try it. She can always come home, any time she wants to," Mama told her.

Happy with Mama's defense of my choice, I was nevertheless surprised that she saw this as a temporary plan. To me, the convent was going to be my home forever, until I died and they wrapped me in a black shroud buried me in the little cemetery on Harlem, under the swaying branches of the green willow trees that no one ever came out to trim, beside the rest of the sisters who had passed from this life. I was looking forward to it. Of course, that would only be after a long life of toil and deprivation, working for Jesus.

Oh, that thought lead me to another thought: I had not said my Holy Hours today, nor my rosary, nor had I gone to Mass this morning because Mama said we had to clean the house before Aunt Esther and Uncle Phil arrived. You would think these prayers and devotions would be second nature to me by now, instead of a chore that must be completed. Jesus is probably going to kick me out of his chosen flock.

I resolved to say the prayers twice tomorrow in order to catch up and be in Jesus' good graces.

Grandma Anna asked me, after Aunt Esther and Uncle Phil had gone home, what I really wanted to do. "Do you really want to be a nun, Sally-baby? Do you think you will like living there in the convent with all those women and not coming home to see your family?"

"Grandma, I have wanted this since I was eleven or twelve years old. You used to encourage me and say that Jesus would be so happy if I became a nun. Why do you ask me now?"

"It didn't seem so final before. Now, you're going away and you won't be my baby anymore. You will be a sister in a black habit, your pretty red hair will be all covered up, and I won't be your grandma," she placed her soft, veiny hand on my cheek.

I squeezed into her arms for a long hug. "We'll be just the same, Grandma. You will still visit me and sometimes nuns get to go home and visit their families.

CHAPTER 11

— ❧ —

Training to be the Bride of Christ

AFTER AUNT ESTHER'S visit in July of 1965, I spent the waning summer weeks collecting the items on the entrance list that the contact sister at the motherhouse gave me when I declared that I wanted to enter the order. The list was long, and many of the items were hard to find. I needed to bring cotton undershirts – a first for me. I thought undershirts were just for men, but when you wear the same woolen dress every day, it is good to have a washable layer between yourself and the garment. I shopped for the items in Sears (white cotton nightgowns) and Thom McCann's (sturdy, lace-up black oxfords with a 2 inch heel, no higher). Somehow, we found the requested plain, black footlocker, about 20" x 20" x 48"; perhaps that was also from Sears. Black stockings, cotton granny panties, shampoo, deodorant, and toiletries to last at least a year were to be purchased and stashed in the footlocker. This trunk was to be brought with us on the day of our entrance into religious life. Poor Papa had to cart it in and deliver it up to big, rough Sr. Ernesta. She carried it down the long hall that I, too, would soon tread to the dormitories.

August 23rd in Chicago is usually a very warm day. If it were on a weekend, people would be crowding the beaches of Lake Michigan. We South-side kids would be packed up and driven to the Indiana sand dunes for a day of sun and swimming, walking barefoot over the dunes and getting stickers in our soles. But this August 23rd was different. This day was chosen to be our first day "in religion". August 23rd is the day that the Catholic Church has dedicated to St, Philip Benizi. He was one of the seven holy men who founded the

Servite Order in Italy and he died on August 23, 1285. The Order chose this day to receive new members as an honor to St. Philip. Six families converged on the tree-covered grounds of the Villa Santa Maria, the training home for postulants and novice sisters of the order of the Servants of Mary, OSM.

Villa Santa Maria is a small estate on the edges of the town of Tinley Park. Right at the entrance there is a beautiful pond shaded by weeping willow, oak, and maple trees. The driveway curves around and you have to go a little way before you see the house which was very long and low, lying across a gentle hill like a reclining cat. You enter into the lower level; a dark hall leads to the common rooms, the refectory, kitchen, and laundry. Upstairs are the chapel, Mother's bedroom, the dormitories, a small kitchenette, a long, airy sun porch and a parlor. Strangely, the front of the house faces into the woods instead of toward the driveway. The sisters acquired it from an estate sale and it suited the purpose of training young women in the religious life very well because it was far away from the distractions of the world and far away from the rest of the convent community. Only the Postulant and Novice Mistress lived there with her charges and with Sister Magdalen as cook. The novices were already installed when we arrived and they stayed out of the way while our parents and families and our baggage piled into the reception room.

The Sowalski family was the first to arrive, so Lois was the first to enter the order. She became the "oldest" in religious life because she was the oldest in age. When we were summoned, Lois had to be the first to appear. When we moved in any kind of line, Lois had to go first. And when we received our habits, she was the first to be invested. If she had known of this rule, Lois would have dawdled at home for a half hour more. She was short, shy and retiring, and being first was painful to her. Next in age was Kathy MacDonald, tall, blond, and fair-skinned, Celtic, of course. Kathy would have been a better choice for First in religion, but God does move mysteriously. I was next oldest, third in religion and relieved to be a follower and not a leader in this new journey. After me, my best friend from eighth grade, Colette Wagner, the one who found it hardest to accept and to obey. Then Nancy Czernik, an earnest Polish girl who had the liveliness of the Energizer Bunny, and then Nancy Hutchings, a tomboy with a Beatles mop of black hair, a trumpet player, outwardly tough but easily bruised. And that was the order in which we faced everything from then onward: eating, cleaning, praying, walking, confessing. Lois always had to do it first and we had to follow in order of our age.

Our Postulant Mistress was an Italian nun who had come to America about 10 years earlier, Sister Mary Leonard. Her English was very good, as was the English of most of the Italian nuns The Servites were a teaching order and so most of these women had been trained as teachers in Italy. The sisters in the kitchen and laundry and sewing room were not teacher-trained, but they tried their best to learn English, sputtering off in Italian when they were stuck for a word or a phrase.

Sr. Leonard's wide face was like a yellow Italian moon gazing everywhere and seeing everything. She stood about five feet, three inches, and her flat-footed walk and her plumpness gave her gravitas. Mostly calm, she sometimes lost all patience with our girlishness and orders to change what we were doing came snapping out of her. When she smiled at our family members, she had an air of old world benevolence; perhaps she was a descendant of the Medicis. When something in our conduct did not measure up, her moony glare concentrated on the offender and caused all of us to seek a place out of range. My strongest impression is her judgmental black eyes searching us out, watching us and weighing us against some rubric that we didn't understand and almost certainly could not measure up to.

None of us ever thought to ask if she was happy with the task of herding around the youngest members of the order. The task was a twenty-four hour job. At the time, I thought she was sixty years old, but looking back, I think she was nearer thirty-eight or forty. Did she miss going to bed at night without worrying what the girls were getting up to? Did she long to be anonymous again, one of the interchangeable sisters sitting in chapel and not keeping a vigilant eye on the twitchy postulants? She, like each of us, had to accept what the Lord, in the guise of Mother Superior Evarista, sent to her. She was now Mother Leonard, but at a certain cost.

After the usual standing in the parlor and chatting nervously, our parents, grandparents, and little and big brothers and sisters finished up their glasses of tea or Tamarindo and came to give us final hugs. The same scene as every other August but with an added bite. This time we were not simply high school girls who lived with the nuns and learned their ways. Now we were starting the measured road toward becoming the spouse of Christ. We were still able to choose home and family but the bonds of religion were pulling tighter. Our indoctrination was becoming more rigorous and our faces were beginning to turn away from the world and all its pomps. Every parent could feel their daughter slipping further away. Mama told me later that the first time she saw my dad cry was after driving home from this farewell. He had tears in his eyes and said to her, "Pearl, I feel we are losing our daughter."

We daughters also felt the increased weight of our convictions pressing down on us. We had to be sure; we had to be right. This was the next step toward giving all up for Jesus.

My own step into religion was hardly informed. Although I was book smart and school smart, I was awkwardly naïve in all other ways. My steps into religion were not driven by mature understanding but by a kind of daredevil decision. The romance of the tall candles flickering into shadows, the recurrent chanting of the high, virginal voices, the swishing of the long black habit, the curve of the veil – black on white, the chance to hide behind an already established form and not to have to forge a personal identity appealed to my mostly introverted nature.

And so, according to convent script, the hugs and kisses were given, the families, sad but somewhat relived to leave the unnerving atmosphere of the convent, filed down the hall to the parking lot and their waiting cars. Some had handkerchiefs pressed to their noses, others – especially the younger siblings – were dancing along, eager to get out of the dim interior and into the August sunshine and the rest of the day.

Among our group, Lois needed a Kleenex, and so did Kathy and Nancy Hutch, although Nancy was a tough girl, athletic and independent. Still, this was her first night in the convent. The rest of us, Nancy Czernik, Colette, and I, were well used to this. We also knew that expressing attachment to family was not a quality to encourage. We were now Christ's family and our allegiance was to him and to his Holy Mother. A little pang of homesickness was allowed but a future bride of Christ will save her tears for the sufferings of Jesus.

There followed a light supper, barely eaten by some of us, then Vespers and the Rosary and a new, strange bed in a new strange home. And, admittedly, a few quiet tears.

CHAPTER 12

———— ❦ ————

5:30 AM and The Little Office

EVERY MORNING, 5:30 am in the winter, 6 am in the summer, the insistent clanging of the old windup alarm clock woke us. In our white cotton nightgowns, we leaped out of bed and fell to our knees for the morning prayer. Half of the group would head to the communal bathroom to wash face, brush teeth, put on deodorant, and take care of other needs. The other half would be in their cubicles, struggling to dress underneath the billowing nightgowns. Even though we were each sheltered by four walls of curtains, it was forbidden to pull the nightgown off and stand naked in our cubicle while we put on bra, panties, socks and shoes, and the black postulant uniform. Modesty first in every situation. So the air was filled with the sound of flapping cotton gowns as we struggled to get everything on straight. Then we in the cubicles changed places with those in the bathroom and finished our ablutions. Almost ready, we put on our black, elbow-length capes and fastened our white celluloid collars and positioned our black net postulant's veil, fastened in place with a couple of bobby pins. In later religious life, we would be stationed at places that had separate bedrooms but right now, in the long room used as a dormitory, modesty was guarded and enforced by a construct of metal pipes on which opaque curtains slid on clattery rings. Each bed was a private haven in the midst of dormitory life.

After half an hour, the designated novice rang another bell for chapel. All six of us headed down the darkened hallway to the small chapel in our religious age order. The novices were always there before us. Wearing the full veil, they didn't have to deal with hair

her about her home life or history she gave a little laugh, watching Mother Leonard at the same time and tossed her head but no stories or opinions came from her. Maybe this was convent policy that no one interferes with the work of the Postulant Mistress in the formation of new religious. Or maybe she didn't have as much English as I thought. If we thought she was not paying attention to us and transgressed in her presence – speaking after Grand Silence or sitting on the steps and chatting instead of cleaning – we were wrong. She promptly went to Mother Leonard and gave her a full report. She was not mean-spirited, just doing what she believed was her duty. I soon learned to avoid underestimating Sister Magdalen.

Still, I think it was a sacrifice for her to do the task assigned to her: cooking for a bunch of young women who had no idea what religious life encompassed. She had to give up the sisterhood of her peers, and the comfort of being in the Italian part of the community. We newbies were all American in our ways and our ideas.

Six postulants, one canonical novice, and three second-year novices lived at the Villa. After a year of Postulancy, one is accepted into the novitiate and the first canonical year begins, a year of cloister and segregation from the world much more intense than we postulants were experiencing. Postulants were allowed to go to college and to go home for a summer visit but after that testing year, one takes temporary vows and becomes a first year novice. The religious training is much more concentrated. The distractions of the world are eliminated. No academic study except perhaps a course in religion, no teaching, no visiting, no television, no secular books. Just prayer, meditation and intense training in the history and practice of the Servite Order. After that cloistered year, the novice makes a decision to leave or go further in religious life. This would involve making temporary vows again for one year. She is still considered a novice but is given the black veil and appears to all the world to be a real nun, but the sisterhood knows who you are and where you are in the journey toward union with Christ.

The canonical novice wears the black habit but she wears a white veil. This difference tells all the nuns that this person is in their year of cloister and study. She is not allowed to go to any of the convent-wide celebrations unless they are religion-based. No movies, no driving except to the doctor, no outside studies or schooling. If families come to visit the rest of us, she has to go into the house and stay separate lest she lose her focus by hearing worldly news and conversations. Her college time is interrupted for a year of prayer and meditation and for the intensive forming of her religious character.

The one canonical novice at the Villa was a puzzle to us. Her name was Sister Dolores LoGalbo. She was older – maybe forty something – and more Italian than American, although she may have been born in America. She was very thin and rather sickly. I can't remember her ever speaking to us postulants once during the whole year. We suspected she was involved some kind of scandal or misbehavior and we never learned the whole story. Sister Delores had been a nun in good standing and then she did something and left the convent, perhaps to join another order. Once in a while, someone would leave the Mantellates and join the Ladysmith Servite order in Wisconsin; that might be what happened. Mother Leonard herself actually left in later years and joined the Ladysmiths for a time, as did Nancy Czernik. Leonard returned to the Mantellates. Nancy eventually went home and married and had children and grandchildren. When Dolores wanted to come back to the Mantellates, she was allowed to, but she had to do her canonical year over again. This was equivalent to working out in God's gym. Got to get your strength back. That is what we pieced together from various little phrases dropped here and there by Mother Leonard.

Spooky was the feeling I got from her. Italian pride does not easily accept being humbled and she gave off a dangerous air, cutting her eyes at us American girls and turning her head away from our overtures of friendship. The scene was akin to a batch of

Golden Retriever puppies trying to make friends with a street-wise German shepherd. I stayed away from her, and I think she liked that just fine. Whenever Mother Evarista came to the Villa to visit us and inspect our progress, Dolores would have a special, closed-door meeting with her. With rampant curiosity, we all wanted to listen at the door but never had the nerve to try. Nancy Czernik would not do it because she had better control of her vices, but Colette and I really had to fight down our evil urges, grab each other by the arm, and walk quickly past that closed door.

Our second year novices were Monica Szwast (Sister Frances), Angie Michor (Sister Andrea), and Kathy Anderson (Sister Edward), all from the Chicagoland area. Monica was quiet and kind and very modest. She would never tell us if she got an A on a paper. She listened patiently to our young complaints and bafflements, seemed to sympathize with us but did not speak against the establishment. She let us understand that we had to adapt to the structure, not the structure to us. Angie Michor was tan and athletic. She looked like it was hard for her to walk around in all the yardage of the habit. Angie had a way of accepting things as they were that encouraged me to do the same. Kathy Anderson was a little scary. She was tall and very thin, finicky and hard to please. I won her favor early in the year when we washed dishes together and she saw me turn the dish over after washing the front and wash the back also. But I lost her favor soon after when I didn't rinse out the dishcloths well enough and hung them up haphazardly to dry.

These three women had to share their second year novitiate and their Novice Mistress with us, six untrained interlopers, providing them some comic relief as we struggled with the rules and especially with the interpretation of the rules.

CHAPTER 13

The Consolations of Philosophy

FIRST BUSINESS OF the week was to get all nine of us registered for classes at the College of St. Francis in Joliet (now University of St. Francis). Someone did this for each of us – we never went through the catalog and decided to take this and that. I ended up with classes in religion, ancient history, world literature, biology, Spanish, and logic. And piano. Not sure why they thought I needed logic class but it ended up being a life changer for me. Had they known, they would have put me in a second religion class instead.

After breakfast, every weekday, we six trainees piled into the convent station wagon along with the black-veil novices and were driven by Sr. Francis or Sr. Andrea or Sr. Edward to the college.

"What time do we leave after class?" asked Lois.

We looked at our schedules to see who had the latest class and the driver said to meet at a certain time in the cafeteria so we could head home. Home – the word still tripped me up. In my mind I saw all of us going to Mama's house on Central Avenue since my folks' home was only about a mile away from the Villa if you walked straight through the forest preserve, but we turned south instead of north and continued on toward Joliet. Driving was always done by the novices, since they were considered more mature than we postulants. Also, I didn't know how to drive. Nancy Hutchings did, of course, and Kathy, and Colette, but they were not offered the chance in those early weeks.

On the way to school the radio was turned off and a studious silence prevailed. Many of us would soon be reading assignments or proofreading papers. On the way back to the Villa after school, Nancy Hutch would pester the driver to turn on the radio and let us listen to some music. Ever resourceful, she had a music major's line of reasoning. "If I take that course in Contemporary Rhythms," she would argue, "I will need to be familiar with recent music." And sometimes the driving sister would relent and let us listen to WLS. So we reaped the benefits of listening to "Mr. Tambourine Man," "My Girl," "Wooly Bully," and "When a Man Loves a Woman." The last one usually got turned off by Sr. Edward who judged it unfit for young women who were going to be spouses of Christ to listen to and sing along with. Edward was rather rigid then.

Religion class was mildly interesting. The years of the Jewish Diaspora was the main content. Colette, Nancy Czernik, and I all had the same class. Spanish III was lively with Dr. Alba, a short, energetic woman and a refugee from Cuba who had snapping black eyes and snapping opinions on all things regarding Fidel Castro. She pointed me out when the class asked what *delgada* meant. I was flattered but didn't let it show. Ancient History was taught by Mr. Oesterreich. Tall and skinny and well into the process of balding, he seemed better suited to be slogging through breaking news stories in a newspaper office than teaching a bevy of teen-aged girls about the Peloponnesian War.

Logic class opened my eyes to disciplined thinking. A creature of sloppy thinking habits, I had always gotten by with making intuitive choices and guesses, backed up by my voracious reading habit. But Logic presented a different way of dealing with ideas. I loved the mathematical structure of syllogisms and their inevitable outcome. I didn't recognize it at the time but I was falling in love with the beautiful, black-haired, Basque teacher, David Goicoechea, also.

My choices of people to have crushes on were always off-center. At the age of seven or eight, I had a crush on the odd uncle on the Danny Thomas show played by Hans Conried. Hans was no one else's sweetie but I loved the literary way he spoke, a pseudo-intellectual on a comedy show. My other crush was on Pernell Roberts who played the educated oldest son on the TV show, Bonanza. A handsome face is a handsome face, but I have always been seduced by the intellect. My nature was, is Magdalenian: let me just sit at the feet of the master and listen.

But this philosopher was something else. He had the talk; he had the physical beauty; he took an interest in this silly, unformed nunling. When we had finished with the classical forms of Logic, David had us reading Kierkegaard's writings about the phenomenology of falling in love. While Kierkegaard was falling in love with his Regine, I was unknowingly falling in love with David.

How can you fall in love without knowing? For one thing, allowing myself to fall in love with a human would invalidate my profession of wanting to be the bride of Christ. Christ doesn't want any half-measures, as our mistress told us many times. You give yourself completely and joyously or you go home and just become a Christian wife and mother. This last was always said with a slight edge of contempt, maybe not contempt, more like pity for those who are unable or unwilling to go the whole way of loving Jesus by giving up the pleasures of the world. Many nuns showed a snarky pleasure in their face when they discussed the sacrifice that the religious life demands. Choosing the less traveled path made them elite in their own eyes, while the masses of regular Christians were living their lives in a less perfect way, giving less of themselves and enjoying the pleasures of greed and lust and gluttony way out of proportion. Sacrifice is sweeter if you can feel superior about it.

So here I was, constructing a dilemma for myself. Was I going to leave this chosen path of chastity and follow a man whom I knew little about, who had not invited me to follow him, and who was married besides? Being seventeen, I believed love had a much higher value than marriage and children so I had no problems with his marriage. It was his, after all, not mine so I would still be doing right by following love. My archetypes had been informed by Tristan and

Isolde, Lancelot and Guinevere, Abelard and Heloise. Marriage was a piffle to those great hearts. How jejune I was, but at a distance of several decades, I recognize a ruthless streak in my character that doesn't come out often, but would have, if tested then.

More important to the geometry of my designs was the fact that I was not invited to take my life in a different direction. David's conversations with me were mostly academic, even if I thought he was personally interested in me. Most of our talk revolved around the religious life I was living and the one he gave up when he left seminary several years earlier.

His office hours were a great temptation to me. Much of my study time was devoted to thinking up legitimate questions about the course work so that I could go up to the teachers' office on the third floor and have a ten minute private chat with David. Often there were other students there, either asking legitimate questions or doing exactly what I was doing – stretching out time with the handsome, dark-haired teacher. They were eventually finished and David looked toward me, sitting on the radiator shelf in the hall.

"Sally," he said with a brilliant smile, tilting his head, "Come in and talk with me for a few minutes. I was thinking about you last night."

Large blush starting at my white celluloid collar and creeping up toward my bangs. He was thinking of me – at night – when he was lying next to his wife! And, oh heavens, he was slouching in an ancient, green, stuffed chair and had tossed one leg over the arm of the chair so that I was viewing his entire trouser area that was usually not viewable. My eyes flew away from his pants to the statue of Blessed Mother on his book shelf. Safe.

Perhaps he registered my discomfort. He straightened up and sat properly in the chair, shaking his suit coat lapels so they lay more smoothly and waving me into his semi-private office space.

"What do you think about Kierkegaard's comparing himself to a ripe grape just timed for bursting when he sees his beloved on the streets of Copenhagen? Do you think that's how people feel when they fall in love? Then what about the falling part of falling in love? The grapes and the falling business don't go well together, do they?" he asked me with a conspiratorial movement of his eyebrows.

Metaphors. Yes. I can do metaphors. In my newfound wisdom about falling in love, I spoke with the confidence that only a seventeen-year-old can pull off. I stepped into the office and leaned against the painted doorpost, books for the next two classes clasped to my chest. "Mr. G," I began. He told us to call him that because his Basque name, like most Basque names, was so hard to grapple with.

"Mr. G, the difference is that the grape that is ripe for bursting will not burst on its own. The beloved has to take it between his or her teeth and bite. There is pain, definitely, but a productive pain that gives value to the lover's energy. The falling down metaphor I see as an action that is one-sided. The poor soul that loves falls down in secret. The beloved does not see or know, so all the energy of love is lost and turned into the energy of despair," I said. More blushing ensued, on my part, not his. I took this question personally, as I took every word he said to me personally.

"An interesting way to look at it. You really think that the lover needs to be bitten? Blood must be draw?"

"If he is a grape," I countered, "he must be bitten or he must shrivel away. Which would you prefer?" How bold I seemed to myself.

"But now, Sally, we also have to wonder about the "energy of despair". Despair seems to be a languid state with no life, no action. Yet you think there is energy there – even the negative of energy caused by the lover having to pull away from love and turn toward despair."

"This negative of energy. I can't wrap my mind around it," I said. "Energy is in everything. Movement and staying still both require a choice and a certain energy, a continuous choosing. We choose despair, it doesn't just fall over our heads like a burka."

I knew I was jabbering but I didn't want the time together or the conversation to end. As I moved to sit down in the opposite chair, the consarned bell ran for classes to change.

"You have a class this hour?" he asked.

I nodded and picked up my books.

Quick goodbyes said, I took my quivering self out into the hall and down the steps to Spanish class. Danger, danger, my head was telling me. This is not what a bride of Christ should feel or should want to feel. But, oh, the wonderful feeling of being alive, every cell and synapse alive, when we were in the same room.

CHAPTER 14

———— ✤ ————

Saturdays and Feast Days and Holy Days

SCHOOL DAY SCHEDULE was all the same: rise early, pray, breakfast, gather books, car ride to Joliet, classes, car ride home, prayers, supper, chores, prayers, go to bed or go downstairs to the common room to study and do your classwork. Nights ended when your homework was ended. Sometimes this would be one or two o'clock in the morning. We were young and could do this, but we were also very sleepy most of the time.

Saturdays were another program. Saturday morning, after prayers, Mass, and breakfast, was devoted to cleaning the Villa top to bottom. I personally never saw a speck of dirt anywhere but nevertheless had to clean diligently. My assignment was the sunroom where we had spiritual reading. The room was about 14 feet wide and twenty-five feet long. The outside wall was made of a bank of windows about five feet high and eight feet long. Each window was completely covered in Venetian blinds. These were not the sleek miniblinds you see today. They were the ancestors of those skinny shades. Once white, they were now an aged alabaster color, two-inch wide vanes with tangled, yellowed cotton cords.

The first time I cleaned the sunroom I dusted the flat surfaces and vacuumed the carpet and thought I was finished.

Not so.

Mother Leonard came by to check on my work. She saw what I did not and smirked her Italian smirk. "So, Giga, you think you are finished? Have you dusted the blinds?" she asked.

Never crossed my mind that someone had to dust all those blinds. That would take hours. But, yes, that is exactly what she expected, and every Saturday, not just spring and fall.

So downstairs I went for rags and a bucket of suds. And a stepladder. And back upstairs to start at the top of the first set, wiping tops and bottoms of vanes, rinsing out the cloth, wiping some more vanes, rinsing out the cloth. Soon my arm was aching, my neck was cricked, and my eyes were full of dust motes. One thing an aspiring Bride of Christ learns early is patience, perseverance, and obedience. Three things, actually.

Another postulant was given the task of washing the pews with Murphy's Oil Soap. It was a new product to me but after the first week, I could recognize that Murphy's Oil Soap fragrance anywhere. It was the under note of the smell of convents everywhere. Washing pews every week seemed excessive to me but perhaps that kept us healthy by vanquishing the germs from all the hands touching the pews.

Outdoor work was done by an Italian couple who lived in a little house on our grounds. The husband was an immigrant named Sabado. He and his wife raised vegetables and shared them with the nuns. In high summer they would bring us heaps of dandelion greens which the Italians liked. They were cleaned and fried up with bacon grease and fed to the postulants. They tasted a little like mustard greens but more bitter. Sabado also brought the cook huge leaves of a plant that I called elephant ears. These too were cooked up and served to us. Sabado rode an ancient mower over the lawns and kept a pen full of chickens. In the evenings, he would sit outside the pen on a big limestone rock with a shotgun in his hand, waiting for a fox who was bothering the chickens. Although his wife was sweet and shy, Sabado gave us girls a good looking over whenever we were near. I didn't like to have to go to his house but was sometimes sent over with a helping of gnocchi or some pieces of cake. He would open the door and look me over with a sneer, take the plate and shut the door abruptly. I hurried back to the Villa.

After about three weeks of school my birthday arrived. Eighteen years old. That morning there was a vase of yellow roses on the altar. Mama and Papa had sent it but, of course, it was not given to me, but given to God. Still, I enjoyed looking at them and knowing my parents were thinking of me. After Matins, Lauds, meditation and Mass, we went down to breakfast and my place was covered in little offerings, hand-made birthday signs and a vase or two of artificial flowers. It was quite festive. The youngest group, which was us postulants, would always do the birthday décor. We were led by Nancy Czernik in these efforts. She was great at crafts and was also very enthusiastic. She would propose more and more ideas and we would carry them out if we could, having very few materials to work with.

There was a Mass card from Mother Leonard which is a card that says a Mass will be said for your intentions. This is Catholic-speak that means the priest will add a short prayer to all the other prayers that includes asking God to grant your intentions. Now your intentions might be anything from good health for your aging grandmother, a child for your barren sister, an A on the essay you just wrote for World History, or the conversion of Russia.

Other gifts were a bookmark with a saint's picture, can't remember whose. Perhaps a new pair of shoelaces for our clunky black shoes. Mostly, we gave each other holy cards. One card had a picture of Saint Matthew whose feastday was on September 21st, my birthday. Always, I was amused by people making pictures of these ancient Jews and most of the time they looked British: sandy-colored hair, blue eyes, pale beards. Jesus also looked incredibly Anglo-Saxon in most representations. This practice was ludicrous. Haven't people been watching the news? Hadn't they seen people from Israel or Yemen or Syria?

Some holy cards were handmade. We were connoisseurs of holy cards and collected sayings of inspiration and then made our own with small squares of cardboard and colored pens, drawing doves or crowns or flowers - whatever the verse specified. When I had to take an art class, I took calligraphy and it turned out to be very useful. I couldn't draw much but I could glue down colored tissue paper into pleasing montages and write out a verse of something. Khalil Ghibran was one of my freshman year discoveries and I stole many of his verses and lettered them on the cards. May his publishers never read this.

Tuesday this was, and no day off for the birthday girl, but I was much cheered by the warmth of my sisters, and went off to school in a good mood with a bouquet of trout lilies that I had picked in the woods around the Villa while I walked there during meditation.

Birthdays were not as special as one's feast day. This is the day set aside by the Church to honor the saint whose name you carry. In modern times in America, it isn't that easy to know who your patron saint is. Sally is a diminutive of Sara, or Sarah who was the wife of Abraham. Sara, being a Jew, has no feast day. Our two Nancys could claim Saint Anne, the mother of Mary, the mother of Jesus, our bridegroom. Kathryn had a saint famous for dying on her very own Catherine Wheel, and Colette and Lois also had patron saints. So they had two special celebrations in a year but I only had my birthday. Perhaps I could have claimed Saint Salvatore of Horta but his feast day was March 18th; usually it was Lent on March 18th. At supper there would be a special cake or dessert in honor of your feast day, but not if your day was during Lent. Besides, St. Salvatore was a great lover of St. Paul who is always very low on my list of people to admire.

Each religious house in our order had an historian whose task was to keep a journal of the happenings of that house. When there were guests, you wrote that in the book at the end of the day. You also wrote if someone was taken ill, went to doctor appointments or hospital, or died. A celebration of any sort must be entered into the history book and any unusual activity such as a visit by an electrician or plumber.

Somehow, the job of historian became mine and I was given the huge journal, filled with yellowed pages and pages of tiny, neat handwriting. This is their first mistake: my handwriting was not tiny, not neat, nor particularly legible. And my attention to the task was so lackadaisical that often I had to ask Kathy or Lois if anyone had been at the house these last couple of weeks.

There came a day in late November when Mother Leonard asked me to fetch the journal as she wanted to look up the last time Mother Evarista had visited us. I happily zipped upstairs, got the old green ledger and zipped back downstairs, delivering it to her hand. Was not worried. I knew that I had recorded Mother Evarista's last visit, September 14th, when she came to see if we new postulants were settled in well and also to get some of our late garden produce, especially tomatoes which were overrunning us.

Sitting in her wing-backed chair in the common room, Mother Leonard paged through the last several pages, her eyes bulging out a little more at each turned sheet.

"Oh, Madonna, what have you done, Giga?" she asked. "Is this the way you write? Nobody can read this chicken scratching."

I made no reply because I knew that none was really wanted. I just kept my eyes on her face to gauge how bad the storm was going to be. All six of us, sitting at the common room table and doing our homework, looked up apprehensively at Mother. When one person was in trouble, you never knew how many more of us were going to be included in the scolding.

After much clucking and heading shaking and Italian expletives, Mother Leonard went to her desk and came back with a slim, very sharp Exacto knife. She deftly cut out the offending pages and handed them to me. "Now you come back here after Vespers and Compline, and you sit and write these pages out neatly so that even a baby can read them. Go slowly and do this with care, Giga, because two hundred years from now, the sisters must be able to read and know what happened in their convent."

And I did. And it took me several hours to finish so my paper for World Lit was quite a bit shorter than it should have been. We had to write about European Art and since I was rushing, as usual, I had nothing to talk about except some holy cards by a Spanish artist. They were very modern and I pasted them right into the essay – with paste. In those days, cut and paste involved actual paste. It was a silly paper but for some reason I got an A on it. Perhaps the teacher was happy to deal with pictures instead of words for a change.

CHAPTER 15

―――――― ❧ ――――――

Home for Christmas

CHRISTMAS WAS APPROACHING and we postulants would be sent to our homes to celebrate with their families. Our main concern was how to bring presents to our parents and siblings when we had nothing. Accepting Poverty as a lifestyle made us rethink our value structure. I knew Mama and Papa and Grandma Anna didn't expect any gifts but custom runs deep and I still felt I should bring something. I rummaged through the gifts that I had received for my birthday. Shoelaces were not a likely gift, but there was a little book about Saint Therese of Lisieux that Mama will like because her confirmation name was Theresa, and a Spiritual Bouquet for Papa. A spiritual bouquet is a card with a promise of prayers that will be said for that person or for that person's intentions, such as getting a better job or being cured of some illness. What Papa was praying for was unknown to me, but the bouquet assured him that I was helping him pray for whatever he wanted. Grandma Anna was getting some holy cards. She always liked the Infant of Prague pictures and I has just the one for her. The Infant of Prague is always shown in an ornate brocaded cape and a jeweled crown. Being Italian, Grandma liked anything decorated to the hilt. The more red velvet and gold braid the better. My brother was away in the Air Force so I was spared the problem of finding a gift for a guy.

I didn't think about it at the time but the family was probably going through the same worry about presents as I was. They didn't know what they could give me for Christmas since I wasn't allowed to keep anything for myself. If something is expressly for you, like a new pair of prescription glasses was given, you show it to the superior and she will give you permission to keep it. I don't remember what I received, perhaps a book or a pair of gloves. Not important. I didn't have any needs that were not being fulfilled.

Christmas passed, not quick enough for me. All that empty time to fill. Reading, practicing piano, preparing meals and cleaning up from meals, going to Jardine's and saying hello to all the workers. The best part of the holiday was sleeping in. If you give me a chance, I can sleep till noon, and I did several times. My parents let me do as I pleased, although Mama asked if I didn't have to go to church every day.

Whoops! I had forgotten about that. The sisters told us we could use the chapel at St. George and attend mass with the sisters teaching there. And I hadn't attended one single mass since I got home. Next morning I was there at the door of the chapel at 7 am, knocking. I knew reports would be made and I was very anxious that no black marks went against my name. My fear of reprimand was stronger than my love of sleeping, so I was at mass at the sisters' chapel every morning until the end of Christmas break. Nancy Czernik and Colette were there also since this was our home parish.

For teachers and students, the year is divided into semesters and semester breaks, and January was back-to-school time.

Courses in Spanish, French, General Psychology, British Lit, Piano performance, and philosophy were on my schedule. And religion, of course. Sr. Helen-Marie taught Metaphysics. She was a Franciscan nun, tall, slim, brown habit, black veil with a white cuff. Class time was filled with the church fathers and their proofs for the existence of God: Augustine, Thomas Aquinas, The proofs all seemed contrived to me, if this, then that and only that. My powers of debate were very small so I was not able to express my state of uneasiness with the proofs as presented. I certainly had to memorize them for the exam but I was still unconvinced.

Time to go home, you might say. But I was vacillating between long-held dogma and newfound doubts. I memorized what I needed to know to pass the class and continued on with my religious life. The steps toward being a Bride of Christ were set and measured and I did nothing overt to interrupt them. Not so much devotion as lack of an alternate plan.

CHAPTER 16

———— ⚛ ————

Playwrights and Musicians

Weeks went by in measured sameness: prayer, classes, study, chores. March 19th brought a little moment of fun – St. Joseph's Day. We always celebrated with a special meal, more talking, maybe a little play.

Plots had to be written in-house and were a collaborative effort. Colette and I did the plot and writing, Nancy Hutch and Lois provided the music, Nancy Czernik and Kathy worked on costumes and props. The second-year novices kept their minds on their college work and left the frivolity to us postulants. The canonical novice ignored us all, as usual.

This year's work was about a young woman who wants to give her life to Jesus but doesn't know how to start. Pretty predictable I guess, but there was a twist. The girl was a Jewess. Now the playwrights were treading unknown ground. Other than our reading of "The Diary of Anne Frank," Colette and I knew no Jews and didn't have a grasp of speech or traditions. If this were happening after "Fiddler on the Roof" came out, we would have done a better job. But we skated by on the notion that the audience of nuns would be very pleased by the Conversion of the Jews, even if it was only one Jew. This is something that is mentioned in certain prayers and is profoundly hoped for by all Catholics.

Nancy Czernik, because she was small, got to be Rachel, the vacillating Jewess. Kathy, who was tallest, played her father and Lois played her nearly silent mother. Mostly Lois just held a handkerchief up to her eyes and pretended to be crying over the loss of her daughter. I played the Prioress of the convent that Rachel was seeking to join. I talked sternly to Rachel's parents about the consequences of interfering with God's work in a person's heart. Colette did the prompting and the props. All the while, Nancy Hutch played mood music on the piano in keeping with the tenor of the scenes. The whole mini-play was a great success and we were commanded to perform it for the sisters at the motherhouse on Easter evening.

Since we went to a Catholic college, the break for Easter was about ten days long. We started our break on a Wednesday so we would have Holy Thursday off, Good Friday, Holy Saturday and Easter and then we would still have break for the entire week after Easter.

The preparation for Holy Week was intense. Nancy C had much to do since she was the assistant to the Sacristan who was Sister Edward. Sister Edward and Nancy got on well together because they were both exacting and willing to spend hours on tiny details. Colette and I were never asked to be Sacristans because we were both slapdash and cavalier, assuming the altar cloths were straight instead of walking to the back of the church to look critically at the arrangement.

Holy Thursday's service was a re-enactment of the Last Supper with readings, and songs. Holy Communion was the focus of the service as it is of every Catholic Mass. Our convent did not do the washing of the feet portion of the service, even though the Pope himself did it. In some large churches, the priest will wash the feet of twelve pre-chosen parishioners to show Jesus' humility, but this event has always been uncomfortable for the washer and the washed. No one wants their priest to see their feet and pour cold water over them. And the same with us. If Sister Leonard decided to wash my feet I would have trouble with the giggles and then I would never be able to look into her face again. Agape was the heart of the service but it ended with the betrayal by Judas. We went silently to bed to think about how we might have acted in Judas' place.

Good Friday was the bleakest day in the church calendar. No ray of light, no sweet music, no smiling in the darkened halls. We spent most of the day in chapel, immersed in the minute by minute contemplation of Christ's sufferings. Each grisly detail was pounded into us by a visiting priest giving 45 minute talks all through the day until we nearly felt each whip lash on our back, each thorn pressed into our scalp, each dragging footstep up to the hill Golgotha felt in our legs. Father gave a homily every three hours. We filled the in-between times with quiet times in our cubicles. We had spiritual reading material especially made for Good Friday with emphasis on how our sinfulness caused the sufferings of the Lord. Repentance was demanded, and I was willing but I could not find sufficient wickedness in my examination of conscience. I must not have looked deep enough.

Holy Saturday, the day before Easter, was filled with preparations. Cleaning, cleaning, cleaning every little square inch of the house. We started right after breakfast, stopped at noon for a short, pick-up lunch because the kitchen, the stove, the refrigerator, the refectory, the floors, the walls, the windows, every single thing had to be scrubbed, rinsed, polished and put back gleaming in time for the midnight Mass.

As it was in the kitchen, so it was in all the other rooms, too. Colette and I were finally allowed to work in the chapel but the work was to scrub the wooden pews down with Murphy's Oil Soap, dry them, and then apply Johnson's Paste Wax and buff them until you could see your face in them. Our arms nearly fell off from all that buffing but I was happier than I was the day before. At least we could move and do something. Good Friday seemed such a long day with hours and hours of meditation and prayers. Saturday was still a day of sorrow and no unnecessary talking was allowed, but we had something to do instead of sitting on the side of our beds and examining our consciences.

Kathy was kept in the laundry for several hours. Sister Andrea was teaching her to shape and starch the white pleated wimples that the professed nuns wore. The wimple served also as a collar and wrapped under the chin and was pulled upward to the top of the head where you pin it together from the top of the head all the way down the back of the neck to the nape. Then one puts on the white coif covering the forehead and ties it with thin tapes at the back of the head. These are then crowned with your black veil with the starchy white lining. Each sister expected a freshly laundered wimple and coif for Easter Sunday and Kathy spent hours working on the pleats, then laying the wimples down to dry on flat surfaces.

As the day slipped toward evening, we began to finish up our chores and put away the brooms and buckets and polishing cloths. Supper was skipped because we were preparing ourselves for the midnight mass of Holy Saturday and needed to fast before taking communion. The professed sisters put on their Sunday habits and scapulars, their fresh white wimples and coifs and their Sunday veils. After cleaning off the grime of cleaning, we postulants scrubbed our celluloid collars with a toothbrush and checked our capes for spots or stains. We, too, put on our Sunday dresses and short black net veils. We adjusted the pleats of our loose dresses and belted them in place.

Time for choir rehearsal since there was no supper. Nancy Hutch played the organ for us and I directed the choir. Sr. Frances, Sr. Andrea, Kathy, and Colette sang the alto parts; Sr. Delores raised a warbley soprano next to Nancy Czernik who had a strong high voice. Sr. Edward, Lois and Mother Leonard filled out the soprano voices.

I had no idea what I was doing but Nancy coached me along from the organ. She was a much more confident musician than I. And of course, the choir was obedient. We practiced the responses for the midnight service and the Easter morning service. We would be singing the hymns in parts and the anthem *Christus Vincit, Christus Regnat*, a very old Latin victory song, with *Regina Coeli, Laetare* as our closing hymn. Queen of Heaven, Rejoice seems to be a strange choice for the day after Mary lost her son but it was the tradition. She was supposed to share in his victory over death. As an order devoted to Mary, we were attuned to all the facets of her life.

After rehearsal, we went to our rooms – or cubicles – and spent the last hour in contemplation. I must confess that I slept, and I think a few of the other postulants did, also. We had been running from early morning and at 9:30 or 10 PM we were pooped out. The sacristans would be checking on last minute details – candles, incense, the white and gold garments that Father Lambert would be using at this time in the liturgical calendar.

At 11:30 I heard stirrings of curtains, rustlings of habits, and scrapings of shoes. Those who slept lightly were readying themselves to greet their spouse in his resurrected glory.

Holy Saturday Vigil is unique among the liturgies in that the entire congregation gathers outside the church, silently, and in the dark. The priest and altar boy kindle a light – either with a flint and rock or with a standard match. They put the flame to a tall, fat candle and enter the darkened church alone. They walk a few feet up the main aisle and stop. The congregation has been shuffling along behind them in the dark and they stop also. The priest then raises the candle over his head and intones, "Lumen Christi." Light of Christ. And the people answer "Deo Gratias." Thanks be to God. The priest moves forward a few yards and does the same, and so do the people. At last, he comes to the front of the aisle where the transcept is and prays aloud for the third time. We answer again. And he places the fat, highly-decorated Christ Candle in its tall stand. That candle will be lit every Sunday during the Easter season as Christ, the Light of the World.

Now came the sonorous Latin responses we had practiced so well. With a lifting of the solemn mood of Lent, we moved into the joyous beginnings of Easter. "Christus Vincit! Christus Regnat!" We sang the anthem with triumph. The cold dark days of penance were over and the sunshine of Easter morning was dawning. Not really dawning, since it was midnight, but metaphorically dawning. We could look forward to a lighter mood in the convent, fewer frowns from Mother Leonard as she observed our callow, awkward behaviors and our worldly ways. More spiritual sunshine seeped into the mix.

Strangely, the journey of the church year, from nativity to Calvary to resurrection affects a strong dynamic on the inner self. We might believe ourselves to be modern sophisticates and well past such medieval trappings, but the effect of liturgy stirs the psyche and we respond. During Advent we share the anticipation of the birth of a baby, even though we know this event happened two thousand years ago. In Lent we dwell on the pain and injustice of the Lord's death and embrace the sorrow and betrayal he experienced. On Easter morning the mood has lifted and faces in the halls are smiling instead of showing the gloomy introspection of Good Friday. Somehow it becomes present and immediate to us in 1966. That's the genius of liturgy. Every movement is designed to play to the masses, and despite our intellectual pretensions, we are all the masses.

After the midnight Mass, we went to sleep for a few hours. Easter morning we slept a little later (7 AM!), and then dressed and got in the cars to go to the Motherhouse in Blue Island for Easter Morning Mass and for breakfast and probably lunch.

The Motherhouse was the focal point of the several convents that the Mantellate Sisters staffed. Mother Evarista lived there and most of the older Italian nuns also lived there. The high school teachers and administrators lived there – the ones who were nuns. All the nuns who are assigned to teach in various parish schools around the Chicagoland area come back to the motherhouse for special occasions: the greater church holy days of Christmas and Easter, special saints' feast days such as the Seven Holy Founders of our order and St. Julianna who founded the female part of the Servites, Mother Superior's feast day of St. Evaristus whose feast day was October 26th, and especially in the summer for retreats. Sometimes a sister will be called for a special spiritual conference with Mother Superior. If a sister has a problem within herself or a problem with her assignment or even with another sister at her post, the sister will request an audience with mother superior. And sometimes the house superior will request that mother superior talk to an erring sister or a troublemaking sister.

However, today was Easter. No problems, no sadness, only joyful greetings and renewing of friendships with sisters from the farther parishes. The best singer, Sister Gesuina, was hebdomadarian that morning. She led the exultant chant of Matins, Lauds and Tierce. The combined voices of sixty happy virgins soared up into the high ceiling. Then the priest entered in his white and gold Easter vestments and the great Easter Mass began. We postulants and novices sang our anthems, *Christus Vincit, Christus Regnat* as prelude and *Regina Coeli, Laetare* during Communion. Tiny Sister Agnes played the organ with gusto, shaking out the dust from the pipes with her crescendos and sforzandos.

Lunch followed, a lovely lunch with a short prayer and then talk and laughter, a chance to visit with Denise and Margaret who were still in the Aspirancy for their Senior year in high school. The folding door panels that divided the professed sisters from the aspirants were opened wide and all could see each other.

The sisters on kitchen duty brought our trays of spaghetti with marvelous sugo, the tomato-based sauce that Italians often call gravy, and trays of golden roasted chicken, big cubes of polenta and more sugo to spoon over them. There was salad and crusty Italian bread. A wonderful feast with even a small glass of red wine for every sister since this was a very special day.

After receiving permission, the sisters chatted merrily in Italian or in English. They exchanged stories about their teaching in the various parish schools, renewing friendships, smiling broadly after forty long days of sadness.

Toward the end of the meal, Mother Evarista asked Sister Addolorata and Sister Antoinette to come into the refectory. She thanked them for the fine dinner and the rest of the sisterhood stood and clapped hands for their labors. Our two cooks probably worked late into the night preparing this meal for sixty or so nuns, and got up early to begin baking chickens and making salads. They were not going to miss Easter Mass but I know they both came in late and sat near the back of the church, leaving as soon as the priest gave the last blessing. They would have missed our final anthem to get the meal put on trays ready for the servers. Their job robbed them of many community moments and I always wondered what they felt about that. Sister Magdalen at the Villa also had to miss some community prayers in order to cook and prepare meals. Even with helpers, the cooks spent most of our prayer time in the kitchens, preparing breakfast, dinner, and supper for us.

One thing the cooks did not miss was our recap of the Conversion of the Jewess play. After a very light and early supper, the entire order gathered in the high school gym and watched my group present the Conversion of the Jewess. Large applause, but they were an easy audience. The aspirants sang some show tunes from My Fair Lady and Mary Poppins with Nancy Hutch playing them on the piano.

After the music, Mother Evarista got up on stage, smiling her scary smile at us all. We postulants were all a little nervous when Mother Evarista was in the room. She was the one who could order our immediate return to our parents' home. That afternoon she had had a longish conference with Sister Leonard and none of us felt confident that we would survive any winnowing of the nunley crop.

Mother said thank you to all the young ones for their hard work on the entertainment, and thank you to the cooks for their fine meals today. And thank you to the Sacristan and Sister Agnes, the organist, for the beautiful preparations for the Easter Mass.

We waited…… and Mother added, "Everyone may sleep in an extra hour tomorrow to rest from their labors." Yay! An extra hour of sleep. It didn't come very often and we were so grateful to hear it.

We all bundled into the station wagon and started the ten mile journey toward Villa Santa Maria. In the far back seat, Nancy and I sang Regina Coeli again, but quietly. Soon Sister Leonard said we should use this half hour to say our rosary and keep our thoughts close to our Lord Jesus, remembering his sacrifices for us. No more singing, just the repetitious chant of the rosary. Today was the Glorious Mysteries: The Resurrection, The Ascension of Jesus into Heaven, The Descent of the Holy Spirit, The Assumption of Mary into Heaven, and The Crowning of Mary as Queen of Heaven and Earth. Nancy and I still wanted to sing, but we pulled out our rosaries and Sister Francetta intoned the Apostles' Creed.

A week off from the College of Saint Francis was very welcome. This was the Catholic college equivalent of Spring Break, but no beer and bikinis at our house. There was extra time for study and assignments that would be due the next week. There was not much left that needed cleaning but we helped Mother Leonard pull out some old boxes from the back of the community room closets, sorting the contents into Put to Use, Put Back in Storage, and Throw Away (the smallest pile). I would have thrown it all away but it was not my call. One box contained six old house history books and I would have liked to read them but they were in a spidery Italian hand, and in Italian. We set those aside to take to the Motherhouse next time we visited.

Some boxes contained the clothes that earlier postulants had been wearing when they arrived at the Villa and religious life. Touching the forsaken clothes brought questions. Is the girl who wore this green plaid skirt and jacket to her first day of religious life still here? What about the owner of this pink satin blouse? Did she stay or was she so homesick that she left before the year was up?

And what did she wear home? Someone else's blouse? Was it easy for her to go home or was it hard to face your relatives and tell them there would be no nun in the family? What did she say the Mother Superior?

As usual, the bell rang for prayer or for lunch and all musings ceased. Still, knowing that someone had already taken that path back to secular life bored pinhole of light in the back of my thoughts.

CHAPTER 17

Wedding Preparations

MONDAY NEXT WAS back to college. Dr. Alba drilled us on Spanish irregular verbs, a paper was due on Alexander Pope for British Lit, and every Monday, Wednesday, and Friday I could sit for fifty minutes under the spell of David Goicoechea.

Our texts for this semester's philosophy course included Martin Buber's "I and Thou" and readings from de Chardin. Looking back, it seems very brave of David to use de Chardin's works in a Catholic college. Much of de Chardin's writings were under severe censure from the Catholic Church because of his controversial views on evolution. The old guard was just not able to encompass de Chardin. But David was.

I looked forward to the lectures when I would be able to hear him speak, and listen to him as he read points to us, and watch him slide back the wing of black hair that dipped forward when he picked up a book or a paper from the low desk. Although I seldom studied for any class, I always studied and read and took notes in David's, because the material was new and difficult, because I wanted to see what he saw in de Chardin's ideas.

David was much more religious and spiritual than I, which was puzzling. I was the one in religious life, so why was he more committed to God? When we talked alone, his spiritual joy bubbled up in every topic. Myself, I was lost in a fog and had nowhere to look for direction.

From experience, I knew that if I raised a question or showed doubt in the little spiritual health checkups we had periodically with Mother Leonard, she would be suspicious of my every word from that point forward. She also would make little barbed comments every chance she got. The 1960's in America were not a comfortable time for the older Italian sisters who were trying to train us in the path that they had been fitted for. We American girls chaffed under the ideal of strict obedience to the rule even when the rule made no sense. We thought it counter-productive to have to ask permission for things that you were given permission for last week. If it was permitted that you could watch the nightly news for your poly-sci class last Friday, why did you have to ask again this Friday? We mostly thought it was to pound us down, while the Italians nuns thought they were building up the virtue of obedience in us.

Both sides were discontented. Mother Leonard seemed more wary of the postulants' intentions. And we postulants, at least I was, were more wary of making a wrong step that would call down the wrath of the institution upon our heads. More importantly, we wanted to be invited to return after the summer break to be initiated as white veil novices. I still wanted to be a Bride of Christ, even if I was dazed by the culture and confused about the spirituality.

The final weeks of freshman year at the College of St. Francis included exams and writing last papers. Most of my papers were written the night before they were due so the pressure was on. Nancy Hutchings was practicing non-stop for her piano exam. Lois, Kathy, and Colette had their heads in their books and I, the queen of disorganization, was typing away as fast as I could go. We only had two typewriters among nine scholars so end of semester was tense with so many of us writing papers.

Sister Magdalen finished up her kitchen work, cleaning and preparing for breakfast, and then popped her head in to the common room downstairs to watch us as we studied and wrote. She shook her head and silently went upstairs to chapel to finish her daily prayers. All that energy spent on books seemed a waste to her. I doubt she had finished grammar school in Italy. She told Mother Leonard that we should be cleaning more and working in the garden now that the weather was good. But Mother told her that we were preparing to be teachers and this was God's will for us at this time, so her grumbling subsided, or rather, went underground. As we walked by, she would mutter about how crazy things were done in America, how training was so much better in her day. Shuffling on her flat, tired feet, she stopped her mumblings when Mother Leonard gave her a look.

Exams went well. And soon it was time to pack up and go home for a two month summer break. The break was for Mother Leonard and Sister Magdalen, I am convinced. Leaving our nest was always uncomfortable for me. Sure, I looked forward to sleeping in past 6 AM and eating anything at any time, and lying around reading books for pleasure. But already the convent had become the normal life and going back "into the world" became an alien movement.

I could feel this awkwardness in my parents, too. They didn't know how to deal with me, what to chat about for two months. When you have an eighteen-year-old around the house, you have to give some thought to schedule: what to do, what to plan. Should we plan a trip somewhere? Should we visit the relatives? Yes, we did that. Went to see Uncle Phil and Aunt Esther in their Chicago brownstone home. Stopped by at Mrs. Anna Ficker's house to tell her about my upcoming ceremony. She had been my Confirmation sponsor and a longtime family friend so I knew she would want to be informed and invited. Stopped at Lee Mager's house. She was my first piano teacher and I wanted to show her what I was doing in music.

For us postulants, our main objective during this two-month sabbatical was really to find a wedding dress that would fit us. I asked my sister-in-law if I could use her dress. Carol had married my brother the year before and still had her dress, all trussed up in tissue and prettily boxed. Mama and I went to Carol's house and I tried it on. After three years of schooling myself to be distant from worldly goods, the frou-frou of a wedding dress was both alien and exciting, and necessary since we were going to have the induction ceremony to become brides of Christ.

CHAPTER 18

Sponsa Christi

THE CEREMONY WAS to be held on August 14, 1966. That meant we had about six weeks to prepare: make guest lists, mail invitations out, go see Sisters Chiarina and Floriana several times for fittings for our new habits which they were already preparing, both an everyday habit and a Sunday habit. The everyday was made of black serge, the Sunday habit of very fine, light-weight wool.

Sharing the big day with Sister Daniel and Sister Stanislaus who were making their perpetual vows, we six were almost giddy with nervousness. Sisters Daniel and Stanislaus were teaching in the parishes for several years. We knew them somewhat but seldom saw them. They were under temporary vows, renewed yearly for three years in a row. Now they had decided to take their perpetual vows and would share the ceremony with us postulants as we became first-year novices, taking the habit and the white first-year veil. Their commitment was much more serious but ours was more interesting to watch: more theater, more drama. We six came back after summer vacation with a nervous resolve to make this life commitment.

As with any major religious step, we began our preparations with a week-long retreat. A priest was engaged to preach the retreat and daily we sat in chapel as he expounded on religious life and its benefits, both temporal and eternal. The two sisters who were making their perpetual vows came to the Villa for the retreat and stayed there for the week. Sister Daniel and Sister Stanislaus kept to themselves, not joining in with our frivolities, subdued as we were. The vows they were contemplating would be a life-long commitment and it was proper for them to prepare their minds and hearts carefully.

After supper, we six postulants would go to the common room and Sister Leonard would read the ritual from the ceremonial book while we walked through the actions so we would not be surprised or make any big goofs.

Mother explained the significance of each part of the ritual. We entered the church in our borrowed wedding gowns to let the assembly know that we were choosing to be the Brides of Christ. Up in the loft, the nuns in the choir would sing, "Veni, Sponsa Christi," Come, Bride of Christ. Each of us walked slowing toward her with our hands steeple-folded in front of us. One by one, we knelt at her knees, pretended to remove our white wedding veils and tilted our heads forward for the part of the ritual where the priest prays that we leave all vanity behind, and then he cuts off our hair. To show how young and foolish I was, I asked Mother Leonard if the priest was going to cut off all of our hair right there at the altar.

"Giga," she said, "you are at the altar, not the barbershop. He is going to cut one piece, not the whole lot. And what difference does it make? You are not going to show your hair again, long or short."

I knew that but was relieved anyway. My hair was my vanity, even if it was covered. More than vanity, my hair was my identity. People always used to stop me and comment on my abundant pile of auburn curls. Without them, I would feel indistinguishable from the rest of the novices. If not for small differences of height and weight, one would find it difficult to tell who was entering or leaving a room. This loss of self was to be desired as one gives their life and work to the Lord but it is a small battlefield for some of us. Lois and some of the others could accept anonymity but Colette and I had more trouble with it. Colette challenged almost everything that was demanded of her. I was too cowardly to challenge out loud but in my head, I argued about some rules that were too alien. Still, it was what the Rule asked of us and we would have to acquiesce and do it with joy and generosity. I resolved to try harder.

Saturday, the day before our transformation, was given to logistics and checking that everything was properly prepared and transported to the Aspirant house. We six would go there Sunday morning. We brought our wedding dresses in their plastic bags down to the common room, checked them for stains or tears and pressed where needed, then hung them from the rafters in the laundry.

Such an extravagance of white silk, satin and lace had never been seen in the Villa. Our group of six was the largest class of postulants in the American chapter of Mantellates and all the older Italian nuns, while wary of the 1960's American girl, were uplifted by the thought that they might finally be starting to grow. Previous years had seen classes of two and three, sometimes only one postulant or none.

Our brand new religious habits were also hung from the tops of doors, making a meditation on vanity by their contrast with the wedding gowns.

After dawn mass on Sunday, we went down to breakfast. Each postulant's place at table was festooned with crepe paper and holy cards portraying the bride/bridegroom theme. We smiled at each other in the breakfast silence and quickly ate. Lead by Mother Leonard, we then gathered up all of our gowns and laid them in the station wagon. Sister Ernesta had come down from the Motherhouse with an empty station wagon to carry us away since the gowns and new habits took up all the space available in our vehicle. We piled inside, chattering away.

"Did you bring your high heels? Did you bring mine? Where are our nun shoes for afterward?"

"I couldn't find my hairbrush!"

"How will we get the dress back to our moms?"

"Sister Ernesta will give them back to your family after the reception."

Little questions that had not worried us for years. We didn't know the organization of the sisters who had put on many, many reception of the habit ceremonies and knew exactly what each step was. Nothing was missing; nothing was forgotten.

Our parents came into the Aspirancy house just before we left for the ceremony. From the mothers, there was exclaiming about the dresses, about the shoes, about our hair. Nancy Czernik's younger sister Kathy had come early and helped us all with our hairdos. The fathers stood awkwardly while the fussing continued. Their job at their daughter's wedding would usually be to have a hard word with the groom but this time that would not be appropriate.

Polaroids and Brownie cameras were employed; pictures were taken. Last minutes whispers between mother or father and daughter: "Do you really want to go on with this? You can still come home, you know? Anytime. Your room is still there waiting for you." A tear dropping from my Papa's eye. Hugs and assurances that "Yes, this is what I want to do. I will be fine. Everything will be fine."

Papa tried one last time to slip a twenty into my palm. I smiled my thanks and took it because I knew he would feel better about this strange – to him – day.

Sister Evarista was in the parlor of the aspirant house, greeting parents, patting them on the back, assuring them their daughters were in God's hands. At this time, she started whisking them down the outside steps, sending them across the asphalt parking lot to the chapel in the high school so they could take their place in the parents' pews.

Nancy Hutch and I were peeking out the music room window. We saw her mom and my mom turn back for a last look at their daughters. I started to wave but Sister Leonard came up behind me and pulled the curtains together. She waved everyone else out of the music room except us six new brides.

"Now it is time to turn your thoughts to your bridegroom, girls," she said to us all. "Quiet your thoughts and put resolve in your hearts to serve your lord and be his obedient and faithful spouse. When they are singing 'Veni, Sponsa Christi' the congregation is inviting you to embrace a life of poverty and chastity and obedience to Jesus. These fancy dresses and high heeled shoes are just to show the world what you are rejecting for His sake. You must keep your resolve in your heart to give everything to Him, everything and every day. Jesus does not want a bride who gives him only 50% or 60% or even 99% of her love and her labor. If you don't want to give Him all, now is the time to say you are finished."

We six stood there in our silk and satin finery and our unaccustomed high heels that were getting to be painful. No one stepped forward to hand back their wedding veil so Mother Leonard lined us up, oldest in religion Lois through youngest, Nancy Hutchings, and we started our short walk to the chapel steps. Six young women dressed in bridal white floating across the lawn toward their lover.

The breeze was trying to steal our veils as we walked across the pavement. As I clutched my veil and little pearly crown, I looked up toward the landing of the chapel steps and there, standing tall and smiling and looking toward me, was the man who was in my thoughts day and night. He had accepted my invitation to come to my reception of the habit ceremony, but I didn't really think he would attend. I thought he was just being polite. Perhaps he had come because he was curious about the ritual, or because he knew all six of us by sight from the college cafeteria. But I was convinced in my heart that he was there for me alone.

I could not meet his eye as I mounted the steps into the chapel, blushing with suppressed joy. Once I reached the top landing, I glanced toward his face and nodded my thanks for him taking the time to share my special day with me. And then I was through the doorway and into the dimness of the chapel, following Kathy MacDonald to our future as brides of Christ.

Several hundred people, parents, brothers and sisters, aunts and uncles of the brides, some specially invited guests like David, and a few strangers to us waited to witness this unusual event. There were young people whom the sisters were trying to persuade into the religious life, a few classmates from St. George Elementary and a few girls from our classes in the high school. All rose when the procession of brides entered and stood while we walked slowly to the first row of seats. Six very young women in white bouffant gowns and fluttering veils. We were ready to pledge our lives to service in the church.

Behind us came Sisters Daniel and Stanislaus, only a few years older in life, but several years older in religion. They were, in truth, the main event. The vows they would take this afternoon were forever. They had already served their canonical novice year and three years of temporary vows. Now they would pledge themselves to this life forever, and their demeanor showed their commitment. No silliness, no smiling at family. Dressed in their full black habits including the overlaying mantel, heads bowed, both Daniel and Stanislaus walked as it wrapped in a cloud of quietness, steadily forward to the altar where they would place their young lives.

Archbishop Cody was standing at the altar to receive us. His white and gold chasuble reflected the glow of candles. Mother Evarista and Mother Leonard lead us six forward to the altar, where we stood in our last worldly display.

As we knelt in a row before the archbishop, Mother removed our wedding veils and prayers were offered for our steadfastness. Archbishop Cody took a large shears in his right hand and held it aloft while saying the prayers that ask for our transformation into God's servant. He beaconed us up the steps one by one to kneel before him and bow our heads as he used the great shears to cut four locks of our hair, tossing the curls into a silver receptacle. He then sent us back to our places at the altar rail while he turned and washed his hands.

At that point, Mother Evarista put her hand under Lois's arm and helped her stand up. Behind each of us stood a professed sister who also helped us rise and walk out of the church by the side door into the sacristy. There they helped us change from our lacey white gowns into the black wool tunic, changing our nylons for the black cotton stockings, and giving up our white heels for the sturdy black shoes that we could do God's work in. Our assigned nun would help us put on the new clothing that was being blessed at this very moment by Archbishop Cody.

While we were getting changed, Sister Daniel and Sister Stanislaus came forward and recited their vows of perpetual poverty, chastity and obedience to the Rule. Their ceremony was not as dramatic as ours, simply two habited nuns, kneeling before the archbishop, placing their hands in his and vowing to give their entire lives to their Lord in service of His church and receiving the cross-shaped ring of the professed sister. We six postulants only agreed that we were "disposed to keep the Statues, Regulations, and Constitutions" of the Mantellate Sisters of the Third Order of the Servants of Mary. But Daniel and Stanislaus were making a vow that could only be broken with a dispensation from the Pope. I was in awe of them and their commitment. Such resolve seemed far in my future.

But as far as drama and pageantry, that would be us postulants.

After a wait of some fifteen minutes, the congregation watched a line of six black-clad young women emerge from the sacristy side door through which six billowing brides had disappeared. We stood at the altar rail like six black storks in our collarless black tunics, hair pinned back so the coif and wimple would fit, with our personal dresser behind each of us. Lois was assisted by Sr. Felicita, the high school principal. Sr. Emilia dressed Kathy, Mother Leonard dressed me. Colette had Sr. Phillip, the librarian, Nancy Czernik had Mother Evarista behind her, and Nancy Hutchings had Sr. Virginia.

The archbishop blessed each piece of our new habits: the robe "that it be a strong armour to cover them against sins;" the cincture "to bind up their limbs that they might serve you loyally when the desires of their flesh are controlled;" the scapular "showing humility of heart and contempt of the world;" the veil "that she who wears it be subject to you in all things."

Six stacks of black wool scapulars and veils were piled on the white altarcloth. After the archbishop read prayers over them, a go-between sister carried each stack of garments from the archbishop and placed them in the competent hands of the dresser. We already wore the tunic and the dresser helped us put on the scapular, the cincture (belt), the coif and wimple, the starched white veil of the canonical first-year novice. We were given the long, wooden rosary that sisters wear on their cincture in order to pray without ceasing and were re-given our Little Office of the Blessed Virgin Mary.

Each dresser worked quickly and silently to garb her charge with little help from the postulant. Theoretically, we girls knew what each item of clothing was but we had no practical experience of how to get into it so there was a good deal of flapping and shrugging and grunting, and a giggle or two. However, this was all shielded from the watching congregation by the bell-shaped silhouettes of our dressers who wore the full habit, including the ground-skimming mantel from which our family of the Servite order takes its name. This garment is a floor-length, black wool cloak, buckled at the throat, and it covers every part of a nun from the neck down to the floor. Seen from the back while the dressers were working hard on us, it would have flared out and hidden everything from the people in the pews.

Mantels are not worn every day. They don't allow much move-ment and a sister cannot do her work in the mantel. Originally they were worn as cloaks against the cold but nuns now wore sweaters and jackets. For ceremonial times, the mantels look graceful and add an atmosphere of significance to the occasion, like the queen changing her hat for her tiara.

Excitement rustled through the church and through our row also. This was the part of the ceremony where we received our new names in religion and our parents were also interested to see what they will be calling their daughters for the rest of their lives. Weeks earlier we were asked to write our choices of three names on a piece of paper, and put them in order of preference. Of course, we already knew that you were not to have any preferences at all, so it seemed a silly thing to do. Still, we each had our hopes about our religious name – what people would call us for the rest of our lives.

I took my paper, thoughts about Sister Uggacchiona slipping through my head. (Oh, please, not some horrible saint's name like that.) Sally is not a saint's name and my mother only got away with naming me Sally because she was going to the Methodist church in Arkansas at the time. She had me baptized there and they do not insist on patron saints. I had asked for Madeleine since I really loved Mary Magdalene and Mary, Martha's sister. My second choice was Faustina. My father's birthday was February 15, the feast day of St. Faustus, and Faustus translated into happy or joyful. Since I was usually pretty joyful and it would honor my dad, I put Faustina down next. Lastly, I asked for Elizabeth, just because I liked it.

Now, the announcement by Archbishop Cody: Lois Sowalski will henceforth be known as Sister Mary Jeanine, Katherine MacDonald will be known as Sister Mary Patrick, Sally Jardine will be known as Sister Mary Faustina.(Well, not Madeleine. We already had a Sister Magdalen and the superiors who choose our names felt that would be too confusing.) Colette Wagner was now known at Sister Mary James; Nancy Czernik as Sister Mary Michelle, and Nancy Hutchings as Sister Mary Mark.

Finally, pushed and pulled rather summarily by the dresser, coifed and clothed in black habit and white veil, we were ready. The only thing lacking was our crown of roses and these were brought forward on white satin pillows by the go-between sister after the archbishop blessed them. As each dresser affixed the circle of pink roses atop our white veils with straight pins, the choir sang again, "Veni, Sponsa Christi, come, thou bride of Jesus Christ, receive this crown, a symbol of that which the Lord has prepared for thee from all eternity."

A tall white candle was lighted at the altar for each of us and placed in our hands with the words, "Receive into thy hands this burning light, a symbol of the good works with which thou shalt forever bless God." Then the dressers melted away into the side aisles and, led by Lois, I mean Sister Jeanine, we turned and faced the congregation, some of whom were smiling, some wiping tears away. All were craning their heads to get a good look at the new nuns.

Slowly heading down the center aisle, one by one in the order of religion, we carried our light before us, out the door and into our new life.

Six little Postulants: 1st row: Nancy Hutchings, Nancy Czernik, Lois Sowalski. 2nd row: Colette Wagner, me, Katherine MacDonald.

Mama and me on Visiting Day at the Villa Santa Maria

David watching the six brides entrance: Lois, Kathy, me, Colette, Nancy C, Nancy H.

Putting away vanity: the symbolic haircutting.

Taking my first steps as Sister Mary Faustina, OSM, followed by Sr. Mary James, Sr. Mary Michelle, and Sr. Mary Mark.

Marrying the sailor: August 29, 1970. Colette,
Rosie, and Nancy H. are my bridesmaids.

Me and the sailor and the shortest skirt.

Reunion with the sisters.
Colette, Denise, Kathy, Lana, Margaret, Regina,
Nancy H., me, Dorothy (Sr. Virginia).

CHAPTER 19

———— ✿ ————

New Troops Arriving

AFTER THE RAZZLE-DAZZLE of the investiture ceremony, the silence of the following morning was the model for the rest of our canonical year. Prayer, meditation, silence, spiritual reading, silence, individual training and counseling with the Novice Mistress who was still Mother Leonard. Silence. And hard physical work. And silence.

First morning was a challenge. For the first time, I had to put all the new clothing parts on by myself. And I had to do it in time for chapel. We all struggled and flapped around in our individual cubicles. The habit and scapular and cincture were easy. It was the wimple and coif that took so much time, gathering all the starchy pleats of the wimple and pinning them together at the back of my neck, then at the back of my head, then at the top of my head. Over my forehead I tied the linen band, two strings at the bottom, two at the top. And on top of all this cloth, I settle my stiff white veil, securing it with long, straight pins right over my ears. You must not poke the pins into your ears because then you will bleed onto your white veil and look horrible for the rest of the week until you get a clean veil on Sunday morning.

There was no mirror so I had to trust that everything was rightly placed and then hurry down the hall for prayers.

We were all assembled in chapel except Nancy Hutchings – Sr. Mark. She was often time-challenged and this morning was no different. She came sliding in about four minutes late, and knelt by Mother Leonard's prie dieu until given permission to go to her place. Permission granted with a nod.

Mother Leonard then rose and walked to the front of the chapel. She stood in front of us, regarding her little flock, and then burst into deep chuckles. "O Jesu," she said, covering her mouth and shaking her head, "look at your new brides. They cannot even get dressed in the morning. How will they do your work?"

She went over to Sr. James and pulled James' scapular straighter. Sr. Patrick's veil was crooked, one side pinned two inches further forward than the other. Mother unpinned Patrick's veil on one side and re-pinned it. She looked at me and pulled my band down an inch over my forehead. The movement allowed a lock of hair to slip out and she stuffed that back out of sight. Lois – Sr. Jeanine – had her belt fastened over her scapular. Mother pulled the scapular out and went back to her place. She picked up her Office and motioned to me to begin the chant for Matins.

And so began our first day as canonical novices.

After breakfast, we had to start moving our beds closer together in the dormitory to accommodate the incoming class of postulants. Denise and Margaret were joined by four young women to form another postulant class of six. The convent was awhirl with plans to squeeze twelve young women into the house. Since our black-veiled novices, Sr. Edward, Sr. Andrea, and Sr. Frances were already moved out and placed in parishes as teachers, that meant only three more beds, three more places at table, three more prie dieux in the chapel.

We novices began to shorten the railings between the beds where our privacy curtains ran on rings and made each cubicle a little smaller. In the bathrooms, old Sabado, the handyman, installed more towel bars but only at a time when all of us were outside. There was no question about being in your bedroom with a man present, even one as ancient and crabby as Sabado.

On August 23rd, Denise and Margaret returned from their last summer at home to the motherhouse to be received as postulants. Then Rose Bradaric arrived with her very blond and beautiful Italian mother and her father, a hefty Chicago policeman known as Big Mike. Regina Zekis, a classically beautiful brunette with smiling eyes, followed Rose. And Lana Coleman who was quiet and skittish as a bunny. Fluffy, too, in her adolescent softness. Last to arrive was a tall, competent-looking young woman, Marianne Talien, from our parish in Hobart, Indiana. Marianne was a sturdy blonde and appeared determined to get started on this nun business as soon as possible.

These six young women were offering their lives to Christ and his work on earth. And hoped to do it through the Mantellate Sisters.

We novices were thinking about the new girls who had to go through the same meeting in the parlor and farewells to family and first meal as my group did a year ago. They would spend their first night in religion at the Aspirancy House in Blue Island and come to the Villa the next morning.

After Morning Prayer, Mass, meditation and breakfast, the station wagons arrived with the new postulants and their foot lockers. Sr. Ernesta and Mother Evarista debouched and the postulants stepped out one by one to view their new home.

Novices were not allowed outside to greet them because of all the bustle. Our minds and hearts were to stay concentrated on our Spouse. Still, we heard all the commotion and knew what was taking place. Kathy and Colette, I mean Sr. Patrick and Sr. James, and I peeked through the venetian blinds in the sunroom to see how the new ones looked. Excitement filled the rooms as we listened to a dozen feet stepping down the hall, going back down to the common room to pick up bundles: school books, ditty bag with personal items, Little Office books and rosaries. Subdued chatting reached us also as the girls asked questions about which room they were assigned and where the bathroom was in relation to their bedroom.

Eventually, all was stowed away to Mother Leonard's satisfaction and it was time for chanting Prime and Tierce. She led the new postulants into the chapel where we white veils were already kneeling and assigned them places that they would keep for the next twelve months, unless they went home sooner. Rose and Marianne toward the back next to me and Sr. Patrick, as they were both tall, Lana and Regina in the middle section by Sr. James (Colette) and Sr. Mark (Nancy Hutchings) and Denise and Margaret up front next to Sr. Michelle (Nancy Czernik) and Sr. Jeanine (Lois). The chapel was fairly small, maybe 20' x 20', and our chants sounded very full and satisfying with so many voices. Of course, Rose, Marianne, Regina and Lana had to be helped since they were new to the Little Office, but their voices bolstered the effect on the places that they were able to sing. As the weeks went by, our chanting became as beautiful as the Motherhouse singing. We were younger and had more air and most of us were pretty good at the Hebdomadarian duty.

In the afternoon, tasks were assigned to all twelve of us. Like a Marine sergeant, Mother Leonard called us together and, consulting her clipboard, gave out the news: Sr. Faustina, Regina and Marianne were assigned the kitchen and common rooms, the basement entry room, and the downstairs bathroom. Sr. Patrick and Rosie were assigned to the laundry. Sr. Michelle, Sr. Jeanine and Denise were assigned the sacristy and the chapel. (Rats. I never get the chapel.) Sr. James, Sr. Mark, and Margaret were assigned the bedrooms and the sunroom. At least I would no longer have to dust thirty feet of venetian blinds. In addition, each of us would take a week of helping Sr. Magdalen in the kitchen, preparing meals with her, serving at table. A team of three was assigned each week to do the perennial dishes. At the Villa, we did not wash our silverware and put it in our drawers as is the custom at the motherhouse. The facilities did not lend themselves to so much to-ing and fro-ing at the Villa, and since the forks and spoons would be few, the dish washing team took care of washing silverware and setting the table for the next meal.

Mother Leonard, in addition to her other duties, ran a preschool for local children. The preschool provided a service to local mothers and also gave the Villa some needed income.

There was a long, concrete block building to the west of the Villa where parents would bring their little ones in the early morning. Mother Leonard greeted them with her big, moon-faced smile and spent four mornings a week playing games, teaching letters and numbers and colors, telling them about Jesus and his family. She was assisted by one or two of us novices. This was not considered a violation of our cloister since we were only talking with children, and not with adults. Children do not yet carry the contagion of the world so contact was allowed.

On preschool mornings, after breakfast, Mother Leonard would choose two of us to work with her at the daycare. Sisters Jeanine, Patrick, Mark, and Michelle were often chosen. Sr. James and I – not as often. I pondered why this was so.

"Colette, we are left behind here again to clean. Why doesn't Mother ask us to work the daycare?"

"I don't know," she replied. "But aren't you glad? I would rather be mopping the common room than mopping up some kid's breakfast."

"Well, yes. I guess so," I said. Neither she nor I were maternal types. Still, I felt rejected.

The best day to be sent to the daycare was Friday. On Fridays, Mother Leonard made spaghetti for her charges' lunch. Her sauce was simple but savory and we novices all wanted to work there on Fridays so we could eat the leftover spaghetti. We filled the small bowls for the children and they dug in, some asking for seconds. On the scarce occasions that I worked there on a Friday, my partner and I looked on nervously. We worried that the kids would eat it all and no leftover for us. But usually there was enough so we could feast on Mother's spaghetti instead of the cheese sandwich and coleslaw that was served in the refectory.

Early September brought another school year. I felt strangely off-kilter. This was the first time since I was five that I was not enrolled in school. The postulants gathered all their books and papers and left in the station wagon, driven by Rose or Regina. After they drove off, the house seemed quietly expectant. Now the schooling of the novitiate began.

Those not involved with daycare spent the mornings keeping the canonical hours, doing spiritual reading and Bible study. Sometime we had a special instruction from a visiting priest or friar on prayer and meditation.

After daycare, Mother Leonard would gather us in the common room and read through the Rule with us, leading discussions on what each vow meant in practical terms. None of us came from wealthy families and some had many siblings so the vow of poverty was not foreign. These were the years before post-modernism gave us several dozen choices of toothpaste and power bars. We had all been raised to skimp and save. No one would have thought to throw away something that could become useful.

CHAPTER 20

I Accuse Myself

THE WORK OF the Novitiate is to train the new class of novices in the meaning of the three Vows that they would soon be making. Mother Church wants workers but she wants informed and willing nuns who have chosen their life mindfully. Every day, after lunch and prayers, Mother led us in reading and discussing the vows. We would pledge ourselves for a period of one year at the end of the canonical year.

Poverty, Mother Leonard explained, is not only about having or not having money. Poverty is living as Christ did, without concern for what you will eat or what you will put on. Poverty is a strong trust in God's power to provide for you all that is needed. In my mind, our convent lives were not lived in poverty. We had everything necessary provided for us. We didn't worry about paying the electricity bill or the grocery bills. We had good clothing, usually good food, decent furnishings, heat when needed, air-conditioning in a few buildings. We had transportation available. I thought of some families who had no idea where their children's next meal would come from and I was embarrassed.

Poverty of spirit was harder to achieve. To live without wanting, to simply accept but not desire anything was going to take me a lifetime to attain. I wanted so many things. I wanted time to read and discuss books and ideas. I wanted to take more college courses. I wanted to do something good for people – teach or serve the poor – somehow make a difference in people's lives. I wanted to sleep in till ten o'clock. I wanted a couch to lie on and a box of chocolates to eat while I read. I wanted to call my time my own and not have to jump up at required intervals to do mandated activities. I wanted to be special to someone and for them to tell me that I was. So much adolescent longing floated in my nineteen-year-old mind. All of it had to go; I was sure of that. We were only to want what our superiors wanted from us. The rest was pride and laziness and misplaced willfulness. Maybe that poverty of spirit would never be mine. Even to desire it was to transgress.

Chastity seemed straightforward. None of the pleasures of the flesh were to get in the way of our mission to love and serve. No boyfriends, no dating, no marriage and no children. Since opportunities to transgress did not seem to be present, I thought chastity would be simple. In this I was also mistaken. A particular practice of chastity was called custody of the eyes. A sister should never gawk about, studying other's faces or just gazing out the windows at passersby. She should be spending her time and thoughts on her bridegroom and her inner life. She especially should not be looking into her sisters' faces for signs of anger or weakness to use as fuel for gossip later. There should be no gossip. Another practice of the virtue of chastity was to keep one's hands inside the opposite sleeve whenever the hands were at rest. Displays of the flesh should be limited to the face only and I think they would gladly have fashioned some type of cover-up for that if it could be made practical.

Obedience was the most complex vow. Occasions to break the vow of obedience were everywhere. You could just be using your judgment in a situation and then find out you were not to use your judgment but were to follow instructions from your superior. How baffling this vow was. How counter-intuitive. Were we not supposed to become adults with good judgment and make mature decisions? How would this happen if we were always acting like little martinets? We saw women in the news who were taking their place in government, medicine, the law and the arts. And we collegiate women were not allowed to decide the smallest detail of our lives.

To make it more confusing, we knew that soon we were going to be charged with the responsibility of teaching a classroom, running parish programs, and becoming superiors of mission convents. So how will we learn to make good decisions if we are kept in childlike submission?

Every month we had Chapter of Faults. This meeting of the household was for the purpose of accusing ourselves and others of failures in following the rule. Usually on a Sunday afternoon, we would gather in the common room, solemn and introspective because we had to come up with something to accuse ourselves of and publicly ask for forgiveness. Also, this was done in order of your age in religion, so quiet Sr. Jeanine had to be the first on her knees in front of the entire group.

Blushing bright red, Jeanine accused herself of talking after Grand Silence and of using a new handkerchief before asking permission. She was reminded by Mother Leonard of the reason we ask for permission for our needs and then told to say an extra rosary and resolve to do better.

Sr. Patrick knelt in the center of the circle of nuns and accused herself of being impatient with a fellow sister and answering her sharply when they were working in the laundry together. She was counseled to remember that all of her sisters are the embodiment of Lord Jesus Christ and should be treated with the same reverence you would give you Lord and Savior. She must say an extra rosary and resolve to do better.

My turn: why was it so easy to watch others confess their faults but so hard to do it yourself? Sinking to my knees in the center of the common room floor, I accused myself of speaking after Grand Silence and of falling asleep during meditation and of questioning my superiors' orders instead of taking them to be Christ's will for me.

Mother Leonard perked up at my admission to questioning her orders.

"What orders did you question, Sister?" she asked me.

"Mother, last Tuesday afternoon I was told to leave my spiritual reading and go to Sabado's house to get some rhubarb for our next breakfast. I said, Yes, Mother," but instead of doing that, I continued reading because I was at the good part of "Kateri Tekakwitha: Mohawk Maid" and thought I could just as easily go to Sabado's house later, during recreation. I thought it was silly to interrupt my reading at that moment when we would be walking outside at supper and I could stop at the cottage and pick up the rhubarb quite easily."

Mother Leonard leaned back in her chair, smiling in that sinister European way, and asked me, "How well did that work, trusting your own judgment instead of your superior's instructions?" She already knew the answer but wanted me to experience a humbling moment.

Still on my knees, I said, "Well, at the end of recreation, when I knocked on Sabado's door, there was no answer. He and his wife had gone into town for her birthday dinner and so, we had no rhubarb for breakfast." I said this with my head lowered and my blushing face hidden behind the starched white veil. I knew for a fact that both Nancys were very pleased not to have rhubarb with their breakfast egg and toast, but this was not the time to bring up that detail.

Mother Leonard used this moment to indulge herself in a mini-sermon on the infinite wisdom of our order's Seven Holy Founders when they wrote the Rule for us to follow. The coldness of the concrete floor overlaid with dark brown, highly-polished composition tiles that I knelt on was seeping up through my knees but I didn't fidget about. Experience taught me to wait patiently while Mother told us the ancient stories of the Founders. After some time, she came to the end of her sermon and said, "Get up, Giga. Say three rosaries for your conscience and resolve to keep our Holy Rule as our Founders meant it."

A sister was supposed to use this time to accuse another of a fault if she observed something wrong, but no one ever did this in our group. It felt like a failure of charity to call someone out and we did so much together that most of us would be implicated. Theoretically, accusing another would help them mend their ways but we just couldn't do it. Too medieval.

Discipline was a word that in convent use was usually preceded by THE. The Discipline was a tool used toward spiritual advancement. The outside world would call it masochistic but nuns and priests saw it as a helper on their journey to sanctity. The Discipline was always to be employed with great restraint and only upon one's self. Never was another sister to inflict the discipline on her peer. Made usually of rope, the discipline was a small whip with seven or nine braided sections. One was to slap oneself on the back or the buttocks with the discipline while saying aloud a prayer. Six or seven lashes were considered enough. Any more and one was in danger of being self-indulgent in a negative manner. The temptation to whip oneself more was seen as a sin of pridefulness. Disciplining the body could turn into a mentally unhealthy obsession, so in the case of physical self-discipline, more was not considered better.

Our order did not use the Discipline but I came across hair shirts in my spiritual readings and asked Mother if I could wear one. A hair shirt is very itchy and is worn in secret, under the clothing, to mortify the flesh and help one think on a higher plane than the bothers of the body. In my nineteen-year-old naiveté, I hoped to impress God with my enthusiasm for suffering but mostly, I hoped to impress Mother Leonard, too. She looked at me over the top of her glasses and said she had never even seen a hair shirt and did not know where we could get one. She did not believe the Mantellates were interested in excessive suffering. If we simply kept the Rule in all of its considered intricacies, we would become that state to be desired, a Living Rule. No one was ever pointed out to us as a Living Rule. There were a few dead nuns remembered as Living Rules but no one alive. Still, we knew the concept and in our fresh hopefulness, we each wanted to become that paragon of virtues. Good to have Ideals.

Being only human, sometimes Mother used this period to illustrate how not to keep your vows with tales of past convents scandals. She told about a sister, many decades ago in Italy, who served breakfast to the visiting priest who said Mass for the convent in Milan. The sister spent much time delivering the eggs and toast and coffee. When her superior came looking for her one day, she found the door to the priest's parlor locked and upon knocking, heard much scuffling and furtive noises. Knocking again, the priest finally poked his head out the door. With his hair all askew he said, "Mother, I am hearing Sr. Jacinta's confession. Pease give us a few minutes." He was not asked back to say Mass again, and Sr. Jacinta spent many long hours in the chapel in prayer with her arms held out cross-like. She would have been sent home in disgrace but her family was a large donor and it seemed wise to help the sister reform herself rather than shame her publically.

Mother Leonard now had two large and disparate assignments given her by the community. She had to train the new postulants in the basic concepts of religious life and she also had to maintain the training and the seclusion of the canonical novice class. Much of the canonical year is mandated by Rome. The Council of Trent itself, in 1545, declared the novitiate should last a full year. Pope Clement VIII demanded that novices should have a time for recreation, both in the house and outdoors. Formal studies were forbidden until 1910 when the Church allowed novices to study languages, the early church writings, and Scriptures so the order could make an assessment of the novices' mental capabilities and their fitness for future work in the Order. Novices also had to make a ten day retreat at the end of their term to prepare for their profession of their vows.

Mother Leonard was a wise and thoughtful person but I never thought she had gone through higher education in Italy. She competently led us through the study of our Servite founders, the Rule and the Vows we would be making, but she was assisted in our other studies by visiting teachers. Sometimes a priest would come out to the Villa and give us a three hour class on a particular topic: St. Paul's epistles, the history of the Early Church, Bible history, moral virtues. Anything pertaining to the spiritual life was allowed and even required so the order could learn the character and capacities of each novice.

We had assignments or tests at the end of the class and a few of the classes were taken for college credit. Most were just formational.

CHAPTER 21

Particular Friendships

WE WHITE VEIL novices took the new postulants under our wings and helped them to understand what was expected. Most of the girls were already friends from the high school or from the aspirancy. Naturally, some people gravitated toward a particular mentor and friendships formed. I was flattered that Rosie seemed to enjoy talking with me. She was pretty much the opposite of me, so I have always been surprised by our friendship. She liked sports and did well in them. She walked with a loose grace, as if her shoulders were being held up by a heavenly coat-hanger and the rest of her swayed from them. In her early years, she watched sports and spent her summers in White Sox Park, Old Comisky Park. With her dad on the police force, she got in to the inner corridors and met lots of players, including her favorite, Luis Aparecio.

Rosie had played drums in our high school orchestra. She was very easy-going and saw humor in everything, often getting in trouble for laughing at some dire pronouncement from her superiors because it struck her as ridiculous. She even laughed during her punishments and would likely come back and give the superior a hug to show that she wasn't mad for being called out.

Rosie amused us all with her easy independent nature, but often she would ask me privately what the reasoning might be behind the directives we were given. I had nothing to say. We just had to do as we were told and assume it was a test of our obedience. I told her I thought Mother Leonard was building our character.

If Rosie was looking down or sad, I found a moment to slide a hand-made holy card into her spiritual reading book. In those days, we copied the graceful art of Sr. Corita Kent whose cards and plaques and banners were sold in all the Catholic stores. Her calligraphy and spare sketches were so modern and cool, in a Catholic way, and we all tried to mimic her style and make our own cards. If Rosie heard me getting called out for some foolishness, she would find a way to sneak into the novice dorm and leave a card showing her solidarity on my pillow. Many times a novice would find a pack of Smarties in her locker as a sweet encouragement. Don't know where the postulants got the Smarties but the kind thoughts helped a lot on a discouraging day. These little acts of friendship were beacons of light in our days. I chose to be in the convent but the minutiae of convent life was so unlike anything in my past life that often my main emotion was bewilderment. A friend to lean on meant you were not alone in your trials and confusions.

Pairing off seemed natural. Sr. Michelle and Denise were compatible because both were serious and dependable. Sr. Jeanine and Margaret connected because Jeanine was timid and Margaret was bossy. Lana and Sr. James were not touchy-feely people so they didn't really bond like some of us but they often paired off anyway for walks and tasks.

Mother Leonard watched her charges carefully for signs of too much intimacy. Our Rule warned sisters to have charity for all and to refrain from spending excessive time with any one sister. I somehow knew the Founders were worried about friendships turning into lesbian relationships. I don't know where my knowledge of this came from; lesbianism was not a subject anyone ever talked about at home and especially not in the convent. Still, it was clear to me that the superiors were vigilant against an outbreak of sisterly-love in the convent. Another reason to keep your distance was to concentrate your longings on Jesus alone and not on other humans.

As December approached, we Novices spent lots of time planning and preparing gifts for Mother and for Sr. Magdalen. It was difficult since we could not go to the store for anything and had no visiting day before Christmas and therefore could not rely on mom or dad to bring us something we could use for a gift. We had to get the postulants to stop at a store after school when they were driving home from Joliet if we needed material or anything else to make the gifts.

The postulants were concerned with their own gift problems. They would be seeing their families and they wanted to give something to parents and little brothers and sisters. Rosie wanted to go shopping and buy something cool for her little brother, Louie, but it was impossible with no money. Since the postulants had Visiting Sunday once a month, perhaps her dad gave her some money as my dad gave me a twenty dollar bill every time. In any case, Louie did get a gift from his sister, and moms and dads had to settle for Spiritual Bouquets.

December was also spent in choir practice for the Christmas service. Once in a great while, local people would come to the Villa for Mass. There was so little room in our chapel now that we were fourteen people plus altar and priest but Christmas might find some visitors there.

I was appointed Choir Mistress and Sr. Mark played the organ for the service. We practiced a lovely Mass setting, Latin of course, and some SSA (first and second soprano and alto) settings of Christmas hymns, since we had enough voices and pretty good singers. Working for half an hour almost every evening, we mastered the music so well that Mother Leonard arranged for us to sing it all again at the Motherhouse on the day after Christmas. An appearance by the young ones made the professed sisters happy. It allowed them to think about continuity. And if we did something well, Mother Leonard made a coup of her own, showing how well she was doing the task assigned her.

Denise, our progressive thinker, was teaching herself to play the guitar and wanted us to sing more modern Christmas songs, such as "Virgin Mary Had a Baby Boy" or "Do You Hear What I Hear?" Mother Leonard had her sing a little of each song and that was the end of that. Not suitable for chapel. Guitar was being used for Mass in some circles but not yet in the Mantellate world. Denise was unhappy about this, arguing that "Silent Night" was written for guitar. Most of us tried to add our support, but there was no recourse except obedience.

We saw changes happening in the church when we were going to college, and we were ready to make those changes. We knew the Mantellates would have to change but we didn't realize how slow the fight would be and how much venom would be spread between the change seekers and the change blockers.

After the holidays, the postulants all went back to school and we novices became more serious in our studies of the vows we would take in August. Actually, to be living with the postulants was already an infraction of the Rule since the canonical novitiate is to be spent in cloister – no contact with the outside world. Here we lived with six lively young women who had most recently been secular and were slowly learning their religious demeanor. We novices were being cheated of our solitude. The long days of silence and prayer and union with God were always interrupted at 3:30 when the boisterous postulants returned from school and slipped their excitement and curiosity and quarrels into our quiet lives.

And I really didn't mind having them there. I loved them individually and liked the feeling of being an older sister. Also, I was tired of spending so many hours alone with God. Prayer was supposed to quiet one's thoughts and to lead one into a receptive state where the voice of God could come through. That waiting stage, where one is an empty vessel waiting for God to fill it, was never mine. When I prayed, the first few sentences were semi-acceptable prayers but the next ones were questions to myself about whether I had completed my work to Mother's satisfaction or what were the others praying for, and the last five minutes of the prayer time were mostly thoughts about how long this seemed. I would get a picture in my mind of all twelve of us mumbling away with our petitions to Jesus and him trying to sort out one prayer from the other.

Praying in itself was an enigma to me. Should I really expect that someone was listening and pondering whether to grant me requests, small and silly as they usually were? And if I simply said "Praise you," wouldn't a superior intelligence get totally bored by that? I mean, how many hosannas would God want to hear from a nineteen-year-old in the Chicago suburbs? To believe that a Supreme Being was listening to one particular human among two billion muttering humans seemed unlikely and impertinent. How prideful the thought was. I had to keep suppressing it.

If one wasn't praising God, one was petitioning God, either for personal goals: more patience, a job for my brother-in-law, passing an exam, or expanded goals: world peace, aid to starving Armenians, wisdom for our leaders. Even the prayer that Jesus taught us to pray is called the seven petitions: may God's name be holy, may his kingdom arrive, may his will be done, give us sustenance, forgive us our evil deeds, keep the devil away from us, and deliver us from evil. Prayer is a gimme, gimme, gimme exercise.

Sometimes I would ask about prayer during our instruction but the answers were the expected ones: God listens to every prayer, God knows you perfectly and will give you what you need, God wants you to talk with him.

"How can we know this?" I would ask. No one seems to answer my prayers, either yea or nay. It's like nobody is out there. As Elijah said of Ba'al, "Perhaps he sleepeth? Or is on a journey?" Well, there is no sense of humor in a Novice Mistress so I gave up on my questioning.

CHAPTER 22

Novices and Boyfriends

As CANONICAL NOVICES, we had no Visiting Day with our families. Our only contact was through letters which we were required to write to our parents at least once a month and could choose to write to friends. We could receive letters from family and friends at any time but all mail coming in and going out was first read by the Novice Mistress. She might have been protecting the Order from bad press by a dissatisfied novice or she might have been protecting the novice from news of a sad nature – grandmother died or father lost his job. In the eyes of the novices, this was old hat. We had been through this in our postulant year, and some of us in our aspirant days.

But to the new postulants, this was outrageous. Regina, Marianne, Rose, and especially Lana were incensed that someone would be reading their letters. They could almost understand that the outgoing mail would be read so nothing objectionable would be said about the nuns, but to read the letters from one's own mother was intolerable.

Well, as we older ones knew, it was tolerable and you would tolerate it – or you would go home.

Visiting Day was preceded by a letter from Rosie's mom telling that they were bringing a young man with them, a friend of Rose and of Sr. Mark.

When Sr. Mark heard this news at recreation, she started and walked away from the group. Mother Leonard noticed this and called Mark to her room later that evening.

"Who is this young man coming with Rosie's parents to visit you, Giga? And why did you get up and leave the common room when you heard this?" Mother was vigilant for her charges and truly concerned by Mark's reaction to the news.

"It's nothing special," Mark replied. "We just used to date when I was a senior. I broke it off back a year ago July when I was sure I was coming to the convent. He had a hard time accepting that. Guys feel you are dumping them for Jesus. And they don't know how to fight that. He's a good guy. He just can't seem to give it up."

Mother Leonard put on her serious face and told Mark that she would not be coming downstairs to help with refreshments on the postulant's Visiting Day. She must stay upstairs and do her classwork or her spiritual reading. She was not to be seen. Especially by the boyfriend.

And so Sr. Mark did. The rest of us were allowed to wander the house as our tasks needed, but Mark had to stay in the dorm or the sunroom or the chapel until the families all left at five o'clock. When supper was over, the postulants were chatting about their families' news. Rose was regaling all of us with a story about her brother Louie's baseball team. She mentioned the name of the boyfriend and how great a particular play he made turned out.

"You shoulda been there, Mark. He really leaped into that ball and turned around and tagged the guy, knocked him to his knees," Rosie said, as if she had been there herself, instead of listened to her brother's recounting.

"We will all go up to Vespers now," Mother Leonard said hastily, rising from her chair.

Boyfriends were out of our lives.

But not so much for me. I still got a letter every three or four months from David, my philosophy teacher. And while he did not pretend to be my boyfriend, the effect of the letters was stirring for me. He wrote as a friend, talking about his travels to Spain and the Netherlands, talking about a phenomenology conference he was attending in Chicago, suggesting books for me to read. Very safe letters but to me there was a secret subtext that I wove under the prosaic. I squeezed every possible ounce of feeling out of the words, re-reading them a hundred times in the privacy of my cell. I kept the postcards and letters in a greeting card box in my nightstand so they were always available. What I expected to develop from the correspondence was unclear but still a delicious possibility.

CHAPTER 23

———— ⌽ ————

Vatican II Presents: Dancing Novices and the Pope Causing an Uproar

CATHOLICS WERE LIVING in difficult times during the 1960s. Pope John 23rd had a vision to open the church to ecumenical thinking, dialogues with other faiths and other philosophies. He challenged the church leaders to "open up the windows" and let the freshness of the Holy Spirit guide them into making the church more contemporary. He rightly understood that the ways of the thirteenth century were finished and modern people needed a more modern expression of faith.

Of course, there were repercussions. Catholics were cozy, dozing in their pews while the priests mumbled Latin prayers to God. And as for talking to Protestants, we were never even allowed to enter their churches, or so our nuns told us in elementary school. Some people in the parishes were rabid about keeping the old forms, holding fast to tradition because "without it, what would we become – Protestants?" Others were excited to try new liturgies that reflected society better. Guitar masses were one way to update the mass. Taking the communion wafer in your hand instead of letting the priest drop it on your tongue was argued to be a more adult and responsible way to approach communion. Like the novices in our convent, the parishioners had always been treated as children who must be shepherded in their journey toward God. The priest was always the mentor and the conduit and parishioners mostly looked on as the priest "performed" the liturgy for them. Protestants did not depend on a pastor to be their lifeline to God; they were able to approach God and shape their relationship as they desired. This was a new concept for Catholics and scared many of them.

The tensions between the Italian upper management and the American workforce in the convent were becoming more apparent to us, even in our novice year. Our superiors were almost all imported from the Italian bosom of our Mantellate Sisters and had been raised in times and a culture quite different from the American 1960s. Also, the freshening breezes of ecumenicalism had never blown through their stuffy, old-world convent. Modernizing two thousand year-old practices was confusing and alarming to the older members. Even changing the priest's location from facing the altar to facing the people was challenging. Thoughtful Catholics were left wondering how far they should be moving toward changes and were the changes proposed always a forward move. Small changes in liturgy were made after much debate and scrutiny. Many found they had to go to Scripture to discover if they were fighting for doctrine or simply for tradition.

Replacing the organ with guitars was one of the more visible changes. Re-writing the Mass and the hymns from Latin to English was also a boondoggle for many. To carry the solemnity and the grace of the Latin language into English was a difficult task and while some people embraced the idea of understanding the liturgy, others wanted it to remain remote and enigmatic. Even today you can find throwback churches that proudly advertise Latin Mass – sixty years after the Second Vatican Council. There is one up the road from me here in Kansas, sixty years after the Second Vatican Council.

Most noticeable in our lives was the change in nuns' attire. We were received into the traditional garb: long habits, long sleeves, neck and head coverings and veil. Sometimes on the news we would see sisters in mid-calf habits without the wimple and coif, with a simple veil and hair showing!

The Mantellate hierarchy was also quite distressed by the Pope's fresh ideas. Nuns are programmed to jump on anything the Pope wishes and put it into practice. But this was awkward. There was no precedent in the Rule for adapting to new societies. You can see this in our very clothing. The habits of most orders of nuns were preset in the 13-1400s and have not changed a whit. No matter that our lives and our work has changed; our habits were the clothing worn by noblewomen in 14th century Europe.

Now the Pope is expecting the sisters to change – to be more consumer friendly – and they were very frightened. The expense – the choices to make – the philosophy behind the changes were debated endlessly.

Our Italian top management attempted to ignore the words of Pope John, but the middle management, American nuns in their thirties and forties – were pushing for modification. They had worked in the classroom in their voluminous black serge habits. They had come home with white chalk all over the wide sleeves and down the front of their scapulars. They had tried to keep an eye on their fractious fifth graders and been hampered by the started wings of their veils. They knew the clothing was not suited to the job. It was hot; it was dusty; it was not clean enough; it had to go.

Many meetings were held at the Motherhouse on Sunday afternoons. Many discussion groups were plotted with preset questions to ponder and debate. Much heat was expended for very little result. The long, hot, medieval habit remained, but sisters were allowed, if their wished, to give up their coif and wimple and wear a modified collar and veil. Sister Floriana was charged with making a couple of models for review. She did this with a heavy heart but as her obedience demanded, two or three "modern" styles veils were modeled by Sr. Gesuina and Sr. Joseph at the next meeting.

Sorry to say, we novices were not invited to these meetings and had little coverage of the debates. We could only imagine the conflict and the comments and the drama. The postulants told us about some of the sisters at the college and their modified outfits. Several had veils that let their hair show. Some had shortened skirts. We were quite smitten by the idea of a different garb, mainly because the habit was so hot and required so much maintenance. As novices we did not expect a change during our canonical year. That would be too much to hope for.

There was a meeting of professional women to do scheduled to be held at our high school, something very unusual. Several of the high school sister were in charge of organizing this event. They wanted to include a modern-ish worship session and Lana heard about the service and asked us six novices to create and perform a liturgical dance.

We had no idea what that meant. Never heard of a liturgical dance and how would it look? Lana volunteered to ask around among the more progressive nuns at the college. She came back with some ideas. We would wear our habits, of course, but we would wear long colorful pastel sashes over our shoulders and would have flags or pennants in matching colors to our sashes. We practiced swooping and turning, always a problem with a veil working as blinders. We fell down and laughed and practiced some more, looking like a group of pandas who had found some fabric scraps and were celebrating their treasure.

On the special day of the event, we danced in the opening procession and swooped and turned while the congregation sang hosannas. Our dance was a success among the visiting sisters. Our own Mantellates were more guarded in their enthusiasm. The younger group liked it; the older power junta looked grim.

The sisters in mission, those who were teaching in parish schools, brought back tales of conflict in their parishes that mirrored the conflict in our order. Many parishioners wanted the old, trusted ways of worship. More importantly, the old trusted way of thinking about God. Other wanted to try new ways. They wanted to use real bread and wine for communion, not just the white wafers. They wanted people in the congregation to play bigger parts in worship and in the details of the parish. The decisions in the schools have always been made by the pastors. People now wanted to have parish councils that actually had some power. Masses said in English and music played on guitars were just bellwether issues. Deep down, the fight was going on for control of the Church. While some priests were willing to share authority, many were not. And they had centuries of tradition to back them up.

In our Mantellate world, these issues mostly split along lines of nationality. The Italian nuns versus the American nuns. Also along lines of age – which came out to about the same division.

Sisters who were teaching often had to go to classes at night in order to finish their degrees. Usually one sister would drive the convent car, taking several others with her to Loyola or DePaul in downtown Chicago to attend night classes. The driver usually had a small sum of money (before credit cards were in common use) in case she needed to buy gas. The others were penniless. If they were hungry, they would have to bring a sandwich with them in a paper bag. If they talked with someone living on the street, they had nothing to share with them except time and prayers, and maybe their supper sandwich. The Order wanted to bill the teachers as professionals but they were still treated like children.

CHAPTER 24

The Final Interview

AUGUST WAS UPON us and our Order always had its ceremonies of reception and profession in August, usually the twenty-second to honor Saint Philip Benizi. The church requires canonical novices to undergo a ten-day retreat before they take their first, temporary vows. We six were spared almost all duties for these ten days. A priest came out to the Villa and gave us talks mornings and afternoons. We chanted every one of the Hours, instead of doing a shortened version. We went for walks, individually, in the surrounding greenery of the forest preserve, meditating on the great step we were about to take. We keep complete silence, except for a short recreation period after lunch and after supper. We had private meetings with our Novice Mistress so she could judge better if we were ready to undertake these vows. And toward the last, we have individual counsels with Mother Evarista. She came out to the Villa to examine us. And we each knew that we were not going anywhere unless Mother Evarista approved of our spiritual state.

Our examinations were in age order so Sr. Jeanine went in to the parlor to speak with Mother Evarista first. She was a timid soul and her eyes were pink with unshed tears before she went it. When she came out, her eyes were red with shed tears, falling down her cheeks and wetting her wimple. The rest of us, waiting on hard chairs in the vestibule, became more apprehensive, if possible. We were in silence and could not comfort Lois or ask what happened. Mother Leonard, sitting with us, told Sr. Jeanine to go to the chapel and spend some time with Jesus. Mother Leonard had no input

143

into the examinations that Mother Evarista carried out. Her input was asked for and given earlier but now she, like us, had to wait and worry six times as we each entered the parlor.

Sr. Patrick was called in next. She stood up straight, looked around at the rest of us, and walked through the dark oak door.

We four who were still waiting were to keep a prayerful silence, practicing custody of the eyes, but we stole glances at each other intermittently. I peeked at Mother Leonard to gauge her thoughts. This was a testing time for her as well as us. She had invested twelve months in forming these six girls. The goal was to mold them into proper Mantellate sisters according to the Rule of Saint Augustine. The finished product should be exactly the same as the finished product of ten years earlier and twenty years earlier. Harder than it seems. If you think about the young women of 1930 or 1940 and compare them to the young women of 1965, you can see that the raw materials are not the same. Young women of the 1960s were larger and stronger due to pre-natal vitamins, personally exposed to so much more controversy and violence and civil unrest through the pervasiveness of television in their childhood. We six were in truth a more docile and less aggressive collection of 1965 graduates than usual, but we had our moments of rebellion and our times of not understanding what was expected and why. Only Sr. James had the courage to push back when she thought an order or a rule was silly. James didn't let Mother Leonard get away with invoking the Rule. She demanded to know why this should be so. She was our bellwether and we could depend on James to ask the questions that the rest of us were afraid to put forward. And she suffered for it. Being out of favor with your superior was painful in a closed community such as ours. James was often the object of Mother Leonard's displeasure, getting frowns and scoldings and cold shoulders turned her way. I loved James for taking the burden of non-conformist. Then I didn't have to do it.

Patrick finally came out of the parlor and it was my turn. I went in slowly, handkerchief tucked in my hand. Mother Evarista sat in a stuffed armchair. On the walnut table to her right was a large black notebook with tiny, crabbed European writing most of the way down the page. Mother turned to a blank page and asked me to sit down. I sat carefully in the wooden chair facing her, keeping my spine straight, my feet planted squarely, and my eyes down. My large rosary make clanking sounds as it settled against the wooden chair leg.

"Sister Faustina," she said, her voice curling around my Italian name with pleasure. "Tell me again why you chose the name Faustina."

This was not the question I was expecting. Pretty easy, so far. I reminded Mother that my father's birthday was February 15th and that was the feast of St. Faustus. Also, I chose it because it means a happy person, and I planned to be happy in the service of the Lord. I might have gone on about how I had really wanted Madeleine for St. Mary Magdalene, but I didn't want to prolong the interview so I lowered my head and waited for the next question.

"But you know, Sister Faustina, don't you, that we must forsake our family and join our lives with Our Lord Jesus, just as He told his followers to leave their father and mother and come follow Him?" she said.

One would think that by now, my fifth year in the structure, I would know better. In the face of Italian bureaucracy, be still, don't argue, bow your head and at least appear to acquiesce, but out of my mouth blurted this: "Yes, Mother, I know that passage but it has always bothered me. It seems rather rude for Jesus to ask us to treat our own family that way, don't you think? Aren't they also part of His family? And if we are to love everyone in Christ, how can we start by rejecting those we already love in favor of strangers? This passage bothers me just like the one at the marriage in Cana. When Mary told Him about the wine being all gone, how could

He tell her, 'Woman, what has that to do with me? My time has not yet come." Even allowing for the differences in cultures, not many mothers would put up with that kind of answer. What could He have meant by that rudeness?"

Her very black eyes focused like spotlights on my face and her very black brows lowered and joined together over the bridge of her nose. I saw too late that my nervous babbling with its implied criticism of Christ's words had led me into dangerous territory.

A lecture followed, which I have mercifully forgotten, but I am sure it centered on the mandate to follow every word that the Lord was reported to have spoken and the foolishness of a nineteen-year-old novice to believe that her interpretation of the Lord's words was valid or acceptable. And how the virtues of humility and obedience should be high on my list of personal goals to be mastered. I was dismissed. I didn't know if she meant from the interview or from the convent. I withdrew from the parlor and closed the big oak door very quietly behind me and sat back down in my chair in the vestibule. Mother Leonard had heard the raised voice of Mother Evarista and, seeing my red cheeks, kindly told me to go to chapel for a while.

We all passed the examen, Mother Leonard told us at supper that night after Mother Evarista and her driver went back to the Motherhouse in Blue Island. Floods of joy and relief, smiles, Sister Jeanine burst into nervous tears. Sister Michelle said "Thank you, Jesus." The postulants were not around to share our relief. They were at the Motherhouse doing a retreat before their reception of the habit. They were practicing wearing their borrowed wedding dresses and high heels, just as we had done twelve months earlier. Talking was allowed at the dinner table that evening, something we canonicals had not been permitted for the past ten days.

Now our ten-day retreat was finished and we had several days to practice the ceremony of temporary vows and to finish sewing our black veils. Sister Floriana came out to the Villa the next morning with yards of beautiful, fine black wool, fabric that gleamed in the overhead light and rippled off the heavy bolt, cascading down the worn oak tables. We cleared off the study table in the common room and she measured out the cloth. With her sharp Italian-made shears, she cut three large squares. Then she cut the squares into two triangles and we sat down with needle and thread to hem the long side and roll the two shorted sides. We had all improved a little since our high-school uniform days so Floriana was not quite so tense, but she still keep her eyes trained on each of us to make sure we did acceptable stitching. She was not going to allow us to make our profession in sloppy veils. Not on her watch.

CHAPTER 25

———— ⌭ ————

Casting a Promise into the Unknown

PROFESSION DAY MORNING. After Mass we once again stuffed ourselves into cars and drove the ten miles to the Motherhouse. The postulants were already there and we all squeezed into the Aspirant House. The three aspirants who lived there would not return from their summer vacation until next week. I looked around the familiar setting, thinking of the three years I spent playing that piano, studying at that table, waiting for my turn in that bathroom. The spiral of time turned tighter and I saw my fifteen-year-old self. She seemed be seeing me, at the same time, smiling at me across the continuum, with a question in her eyes. How I wanted to tell her that she was alright, everything would be alright; don't be hobbled by fear or doubts, just be joyous and be your best self. The hierarchy would adjust. They had to embrace us because we were their future. But the vision passed.

Sunday afternoon and all our families and friends gathered again at the Motherhouse. This time the spotlight was on the postulants in their white wedding gowns as they received the habit.

Rosie's mother and dad were there; her blond, Italian mother looking beautiful in a silk suit, her dad, Big Mike swelling even bigger with pride. My parents, too, and Grandma Anna and uncles and aunts and cousins from Chicago. Twelve families for twelve participants: six of us receiving the habit, six of my class making our first temporary vows. The Mantellates, at least the Mantellates in America, had never seen such an increase in their labor force. The sisters were full of hope that finally they were drawing young women to serve Christ. Sacristans had prepared the altar with cut flowers and the piles of new habits and veils for the six postulants to put on and with six black veils for my class to change into. Twelve long, white candles for us to carry our light out into the world. Sister Addolorata and Sister Antoinette giddily prepared food and more food and beverages for the crowd: cakes and cookies, Tamarindo, tea, coffee. Elder sisters smiling at their own secret reminiscences as they helped arrange the tables with white cloths and more cut flowers. Twelve separate tables were set and decorated: one for each of the celebrants to receive the gifts that families and friends brought – each had a decorated basket for cards filled with good wishes and sometimes a little money for the nuns.

Sister Agnes played pastorales on the organ as the congregation gathered. Then when it was time for the postulants to process in, she switched to the traditional "Veni, Sponsa Christi" and the small choir of nuns up in the loft lifted their silvery voices. Six young women in wedding gowns. Followed by six young women in black habits and white veils. All twelve very serious and very nervous. No one wanted to be the first to make a faux pas.

After the postulants had their haircuts and answered the bishop's questions, they retired to the sacristy to change into the basic habit. We novices moved up to the altar rail and knelt down. The bishop asked us several scripted questions about our willingness to take our vows and our understanding of what the vows meant. Soon we were approaching the altar, one by one, kneeling at the bishop's knees and placing our hands into his as we spoke our vows of poverty, chastity, and obedience for one year. So simple and yet a tremendous alteration in the way we had lived up to this day. We had been under no obligation to live the Rule but now we willingly placed ourselves under this structure, promising to live by an injunction written five hundred years ago. Our whole canonical year had been spent in formation of the understanding of the vows and now we actually spoke them, aloud and in front of the bishop, the sisters of the order and our families and friends. After speaking the words of profession, a chill went down my back and I rose up from the feet of the bishop and went back to my place at the altar rail. The postulants came back out but I hardly noticed the rest of the ceremony. My thoughts were roiling around what I had just promised and how those promises would become a life – the rest of my life.

Later, we went down to the high school cafeteria to greet family and guests. We six looked at each other with new eyes. We had traveled so long together and now we were "real" nuns. Real novices, actually, but we looked like real nuns. Now we could dissolve into the congregation instead of standing out because of our clothing. But everyone in the habit knew even from the back view who everyone else was. The public sees us mostly the same but small differences in shoulder width, height, girth, posture, hand movement, gait, and attitude make each nun recognizable even from far away. But like a colony of penguins or dolphins, we knew who was whom. I suspected that we would still be under the scrutiny of the elders. One cannot rest easy until one is accepted for final vows and becomes a fully professed sister. After final profession, only God can send you home.

CHAPTER 26

❦

Six Nuns in a Station Wagon - Reprise

OUR PRACTICAL FOCUS after taking our temporary vows was on enrolling again in College of Saint Francis. We were all sophomores now, taking the rest of the general courses we needed for our degrees. The big change was our move, all six of us, to Plainfield, Illinois.

The Mantellates had purchased a property – just a two story, wood frame house and a long, low, fishing shack and some acreage with a small pond on it – from a family in Plainfield, a small rural town about twenty miles south of the Villa Santa Maria that had been our home for two years now. The first purpose of the Plainfield house was for those who were attending St Francis to have a home nearby, saving gas and saving travel time. Our group was the first to live there. We spent many, many hours cleaning and painting the house and moving things around. Considering nuns have very little in the way of possessions, it still took much labor to get the six of us and Sister Evarista and Sister Biagina installed.

Six slender single beds were shoved into two bedrooms upstairs. All shared the same small bathroom but Sabado was not here to install towel bars so we had to take our damp towels back to the bedroom and hang them over our headboards to dry. Sister Evarista was placed in the ground floor bedroom- converted from a dining room - and Sister Biagina had her tiny, private room in a little pantry area. We removed half of the shelves and squeezed a bed in there. She put her meager belongings on the other shelves and hung up her picture of Jesus. She was snug and happy. She was always happy and we started to love her right away.

Biagina was our housekeeper, our cook, and our angel. When one of us was down-hearted, Sr. Biagina would sit down by her and tell a story about her youth in Sicily, complete with goats and mandolins. She would recount how crazy the young girls were for Rudolph Valentino, and would sing us a little snatch of song about how *"Rudolpho Valentino e un gran' artisto,"* in work and in love he was Primo. After the tune she looked at us from the side of her eyes, laughing when we exploded into objections about her singing love songs. Very short and dark, she was known for her plump cheeks and her beautiful heart. She saved several of us from despair that year with the warmth of her kindness.

Sister Evarista was our superior, a fact which struck terror into most of us. She was no longer Mother Superior of the American sector of the Mantellates. Someone else took over the rotations, but she was now given charge of our formation in the novitiate and of developing Plainfield into a strong Mantellate presence in the Joliet area. The Plainfield property was started as a convent home for sisters going to college in Joliet but they had great dreams of furthering their mission in the area. Sister Evarista was the best choice for this because she was an excellent fundraiser, schmoozing with wealthy Catholics and helping them be generous in the Lord's cause. She took me with her once to visit the home of the people who sold us the property on Drauden Road. I am sure she expected me to listen and learn from the master. I listened but was so put off by the blatancy of her begging methods that I was no help to her at all. I mostly sat at the people's dining table with my eyes cast down, nodding my head whenever it seemed she was addressing me for backup. I was too young and too American for this type of fundraising. Other novices were taken along on other fundraising occasions and we were consistent in our dislike for the method. Of course, Mother Evarista was disgusted with us and from her point of view, we were worthless, but we were also window-dressing to show the Catholics that young women were indeed entering Christ's service and the need for financial support was great. I can sympathize with her from the distance of time: she had to establish this mission and get it funded. My idea of fundraising was more on the bake sale style and hers was on the endowment style. Hers was much more practical and in her defense, she succeeded.

Time for college enrollment. My schedule included more Spanish, more French, more literature, more science, more history and more piano. The schedule had no philosophy because my dear friend David had moved to Canada and was teaching at Brock University. We corresponded but I missed seeing him at the college and having talks in his office. Distance is a cooling breeze. My white-hot ardor began to cool down to a livable temperature and I was able to think about my studies and my convent life without the daily distraction of seeing him and making up questions, excuses to visit him.

Our new postulants were Leona Biela, a dark and darling young girl from Chicago, Margaret Spagnola, slender and nervous, and Kathleen Hecmovich, a tall graceful girl who came from our school in Hobart, Indiana. The fact that there were only three postulants worried the superiors of our order. They had begun to be used to classes of six girls and three seemed a step backwards toward obscurity but we must accept what the Lord sends us, they would say. The postulants had to drive from their quarters at the Villa Santa Maria for their college classes as we could not fit one more person into the Plainfield house.

What fun it was to be the older, experienced group. That also meant we were in charge of the radio! Our travel time was curtailed since we now lived so close to Joliet; still, we got in many minutes of music. I was not a driver yet but Sr. Michelle, Sr. James, Sr. Mark and Sr. Patrick drove us competently. I was just as pleased to have the time to read. All of my courses had tons of reading assigned, except piano and that had tons of practice hours assigned. Sr. Mark and I took piano and sometimes had to ask everyone to stay a little longer while we used the practice rooms. No complaints – I loved college.

When I filled my time with studies, I didn't have time - I didn't make time - to think about my convent life. More and more, I was finding myself annoyed by the amount of prayer we were expected to make room for in our schedule. We still had Mass and meditation and singing the Office for nearly two hours in the morning. We were expected to make up the noon and afternoon office and the rosary on our own time. Once home, we sang Vespers and Compline together, usually after supper. Then we went to the little fishing shack and did our coursework.

In her "formation" talks with us each evening, Sister Evarista spoke of prayer as an oasis from the heat of the daily world and its difficulties. I tried not to meet her eyes because she was sure to read how many rosaries I was in arrears. Always, I thought I would catch up by saying two rosaries tomorrow since I missed the one for today. Soon it was four and five and nine rosaries in arrears and I had to give up and start fresh. I just didn't see the value of repetition. How could God bear to listen to us all repeating and repeating those words? And why would He want to?

The habit of prayer was leaching away. The interior need for prayer was missing. I knew this was a problem and chose to ignore it at this time.

CHAPTER 27

The Little Lake and the Little Boat

OUR PLAINFIELD PROPERTY encompassed a small lake, not much more than half an acre. There were fish in it because the previous owners had salted it with fingerlings. Sr. Biagina came out with her fishing pole after breakfast was cleared away and stood on the flat shore, flipping out her line with hope and assurance.

She fretted about all the fish she imagined swimming around with grins on their fishy lips. Some days she would catch a fish or two but mostly she got little baby fish and had to toss them back in to grow bigger.

After supper one evening, while we studied at long tables in the ill-named fish house, Biagina and Sister Evarista sat in Adirondack chairs with needlework on their laps. With her characteristic confident smile, Biagina said, "Mother, we need a little boat so I can get out to the middle of the lake where the fish are staying. They don't come by the shore because the water is so shallow and the sun makes the water too hot." Sr. Biagina nodded and waggled her Italian eyebrows at Sister: "Maybe someone has an old, tired boat they could give to us. A little one."

Because we loved her, we all thought hard about where to get a boat. Finally I said I would just ask my parents for a boat. They always cheerfully brought anything I asked for so maybe a boat would be within the range of reasonable requests. Naïveté just oozed out of me in those days.

Next Visiting Day I walked with Mama and Papa around the tiny lake and talked about how Biagina wants to catch fish for our supper but needs to get out into the middle to find them. "Papa, do you know anyone who has an old boat they don't want anymore, a small one of course?"

He said he would think on it and ask around. Since they ran a restaurant and saw hundreds of people every week, many of them regulars and friends, I was sure he would come up with something.

As the year slipped through a very warm autumn toward the semester break, our Sister James became more moody and silent. She would spend much time at school talking with a friend she had made – a lay woman. Fraternizing with lay students was strongly discouraged but no one told Sister Evarista. Sister James' time at our chosen study table was shorter. In the car going home she seldom talked anymore, keeping her thoughts to herself. She was smart, book smart, but taciturn. A broody Irishwoman. I wondered what was going on but Sr. James was very private and would not open up to me so I avoided confronting her with questions.

Sr. James and I had a long-term friendship, starting when she came to our school district in eighth grade. She lived a block or so further from school than I did so she would pick me up at my street and we walked to school together, talking about our common bond, books. At thirteen, reading was a consuming passion for me. At all possible moments, I had a book in front of me, even while ironing or vacuuming. So to meet a friend who wanted to talk about books was special. Most of the girls in class were blossoming into puberty and wanted to talk about the dangerous topics of boys and dates and touching and kissing. But Sr. James (Colette at the time) provided a safe, enjoyable friendship. We continued to be buddies throughout our convent training years but now something different was going on in Sr. James and I did not ask the right questions or did not have the courage to break through her reticence to find out what she was thinking. I had a suspicion that she was getting ready to fly away.

We had been trained from early on not to ask questions about those who left the convent. No announcements were made when a sister left. The superiors would meet privately and be told so that her place in the classroom could be filled. All we could discern was that the sister no longer came to the motherhouse celebrations of Easter or Christmas or retreat. Usually it took several months for us to confirm that one sister was missing. We would whisper among ourselves – "Where is Sister_____? Have you seen her? Is she sick? She wasn't at retreat last July, and she wasn't at Seven Holy Founders' Day in August. Did she leave? Why didn't she say goodbye to us?"

If we were overheard whispering, we would be reprimanded and sent off in various directions to keep us from further collusion. We knew only what "they" wanted us to know.

But it was different with Sr. James. She was right here in our midst. She sat next to me at table, drove the car to school with the rest of us in the passenger seats. And she was slipping away.

I didn't ask her directly and she didn't tell me directly. Something I regret always.

As the weather lightened and spring started pushing her way into the Plains states, we thought again about the little lake and the need for a boat. Biagina got out her poles and hooks and gently pestered our superior about the fishing quandary. Sister Evarista tried to be patient but sometimes had to say, "Sister, please stop all this talking about fish and boats. We must make do with what the Lord provides us. And do it joyfully!" she said with those dark brows drawn together to emphasize that she was finished with the topic.

When Visiting Sunday arrived, my mom and dad drove in the long driveway pulling a trailer behind their station wagon. We all tumbled out of the fish house with curious faces. And there was our boat. It was just a little aluminum boat about eight feet long, with two metal slabs attached to the sidewalls for sitting. There was two oars and two life jackets too. Mama told me later, "I told your father I was not going to be responsible for nuns falling into the lake and drowning in their heavy black clothes." So he had to go find life jackets or buy them for us. Poor Papa.

While he drove to the lakeside and turned around to send the trailer water ward, we sisters clustered at the water's edge, smiling and waving our hands, shouting "Back" and "More, back more," and "Stop" when he was close enough. And then our little boat was released and slipped smoothly into the lake, floating like a leaf while Sr. James held onto its rope so it couldn't get away from us.

Biagina's smile was priceless. She clapped her hands in her guileless way and looked like a child on Christmas morning. Sister Evarista stood still, squinting at the boat, assessing its water-worthiness. Then she remembered herself and came over to Mama and Papa, thanking them for their kindness in providing such a wonderful gift for us.

Sr. Biagina was all for getting out her fishing poles and heading toward the middle but Mother said 'Not on Sunday, Sister. We do not work on God's holy day." But she did allow us to get in the boat, two at a time, since there were two life jackets, and row ourselves around the water for fifteen or twenty minutes each. Sr. Mark took Sr. Biagina out on the boat's maiden voyage. We didn't think the dear lady could contain herself waiting for a turn. Mark even ran into the fish house/community room and got a cushion for her to sit on instead of the cold metal seat. I, of course, stayed on shore and visited with my parents, thanking them again for the boat and all. I was surprised that it was new. Papa said nobody had an old one that they wanted to get rid of so he got out the Sears catalog and found this one. He was always very generous to the house I lived in. With my brother gone to the Air Force and no other children at home, we nuns became a focus for his kindness.

Mama and Papa seemed finally to be accepting my choice of lifestyle. Earlier in the year, per my request, Papa and one of the young bartenders from the restaurant brought out my mahogany piano so that we could play music during our services and so Sr. Mark and I could practice at home. Two busboys from the restaurant came down to Plainfield with Papa and wrestled the piano off the back of a pickup truck. They put it in the chapel room of the house and Sr. Mark and I breathed much better. Neither of us liked being in a home without a piano.

CHAPTER 28

The Ice Cream Incident

THE WARM GLOW of the boat episode lasted for several days but it was illusory because we young ones kept getting into unforeseeable trouble from the lack of cross-cultural understanding of the Old World convent training methods. Our usual hot water existence came to a boiling point over an ice cream cone.

We had Visitation Sunday in early April and my dad slipped another twenty dollar bill into my hand, "in case you need something." I thanked him and put the twenty in my pocket. We said our goodbyes then and after the families left, we all bundled into the convent station wagon and headed to Blue Island and the Motherhouse. The weather was hot and sticky, warmer than the date called for and being stuffed into vehicles without air conditioners was making us all crabby. The reason for the gathering was the Annual Chapter Meeting and every professed sister was obliged to be there. We second year novices were brought along like a bunch of children who could not be left home alone, even though it would have been more productive to leave us home to study for Monday's classes. Not surprisingly, school matters were always secondary to convent matters. The first year novices also were brought from the Villa to the motherhouse.

After supper was cleared, the second year novices were on our own for a couple of hours. The professed nuns would be occupied with Chapter of Faults for a long time. Each sister had to come forward and kneel in the center of the room on the hard wooden floor and tell her faults to the community. Then Mother Evarista would say a few words to the sister and bid her to amend her life.

No absolution since these were faults and not sins. And besides, priests are the only ones who can channel God's forgiveness.

So, what to do on a Sunday evening in spring? As usual, we had our textbooks with us but no one was very interested in a study hour. A brilliant idea shimmered in my forehead and I finally broached the thought.

"I have a twenty dollar bill that my dad gave me, in case I needed anything. Don't you think we need some ice cream?"

I said it in a joking manner just in case I got shot down. The other five looked at each other. We all knew this was not acceptable behavior and we knew that we would be in trouble if anyone found out. But everyone was in Chapter except little Sister Mary, so who would find out? And it's only an ice cream cone.

Sr. Michelle and Sr. Jeanine were the voices against the ice cream but when James, Mark, and Patrick, and I showed our determination to get the cones, Michelle and Jeanine caved in. It really was a hot, sticky evening.

We trooped out to the parking lot. Sr. Michelle drove. She was the only driver whom Mother Evarista trusted. Off we went to Blue Island's downtown in search of soft serve and dipped cones. How tall they were and cold and shimmery on the tongue. Guilt was still in the back of our thoughts, but creamy goodness was in front of us. Repercussions be damned.

And repercussions there were. Mother Evarista did learn that her charges went off in the Villa station wagon and were gone for about an hour, parking the car in the same spot when they returned. We had forgotten that the kitchen sisters were always needed in the kitchen, even after supper. They had to prepare for breakfast before they went to bed so they would make their Chapter of Faults first and then leave to fulfill their duties. Sister Addolorata was not very curious but Sister Antoinette had radar in her nose. She noticed the car was gone and she noticed later it was back in place. If every sister was in Chapter, that left only the novices to drive the car.

Our blast of fun ended in a lecture that burned our ears and a shunning by Mother Evarista for many days after. Our ride home in the station wagon was more subdued than usual. Mother told Patrick to start the rosary and she obediently did so.

Several days of uncomfortable quiet followed. We were all glad to go back to school so we could have six or seven hours of happy encounters. Each evening, on the ride home to the Plainfield house, the gloom began to settle upon us. Mother Evarista spoke with animation to Sister Biagina, but it was total silence toward us novices. On the next Sunday afternoon, Sr. Jeanine was called in to Mother's room for a spiritual chat. We had these every month or two so Mother could assess our growth and development.

After about twenty minutes, Jeanine came out. We could see that she has been crying. When questioned, she just shook her head. Probably she was told not to say anything to us, and she was resolved to follow that instruction. Next was Michelle and James. Michelle came out looking chastened, but James, ever the Irish revolutionary, looked mad. My turn now.

I went in and knelt before Mother Evarista as we are bid. She told me to get up and sit opposite her. Her sermon was predictable: What were you thinking? What made you think you could use convent resources for private use?

"But Mother," I interrupted unwisely, "my dad gave me that money to use as I wished. And it was just an ice cream cone."

That bit of insubordination earned me about fifteen more minutes of sermon that the others had endured. By the end of the conference, I realized the ice cream incident was much more significant to the Italians than it was to the Americans. And I realized there was an even wider philosophical gulf between our two factions than ever before. Always, it had been hard to predict what would make our superiors upset, and now we had another episode to contemplate. Six ice cream cones and one $20 bill. Who could have known the trouble that would come from them?

CHAPTER 29

Our First Casualty

WE STUDIED CONSCIENTIOUSLY, prayed hard, and tried to please Mother Evarista as much as possible. Still, the atmosphere in the house was one of contained panic. Our superior's expectations of us were never satisfied. She called us in separately for counseling, whether we wanted or no. Her talks with me were always about using the gifts that Jesus gave me – being more forward, volunteering to do things. I mumbled my agreement, but resolved not to do that. Whenever I did something new I got in trouble for acting on my own initiative.

Sister James' private talks with Mother Evarista always ended with James' coming out in a very bad mood. She worried all of us but no one seemed able to ask her what the trouble was. At school James still spent a lot of time talking with a lay person, one of the young women going to St. Francis. We all knew we were supposed to go to our superior about this lay friendship, but none of us really wanted to seek her counsel. Perhaps Sister Michelle would because she was very friendly and could get along well with just about anyone. Sister Mark often came out in tears. Not me – I would never give my superior the satisfaction of showing my hurt feelings. Most of us shied away from Mother Evarista like nervous young horses.

April appeared with blooming crabapple trees, crocuses and daffodils popping up in our yard. We prepared our minds for the end of Lent: Holy week and Easter. Sister Mark rehearsed us in the liturgical music. We would be going to St. Mary's, the local parish in

Joliet for Holy Week, but Holy Saturday evening and Easter morning would be at the motherhouse in Blue Island.

We all were excited because the white veil novices would be coming from their cloister time at Villa Santa Maria to share the Eastertide relaxation with us. Canonical novices were not allowed to communicate with the regular nun population but we black veil novices didn't count because we were not yet professed sisters. We have not taken permanent vows yet.

I was anxious to see the younger novices, Denise and Rosie, Regina, Lana, and Margaret and Mary Anne. They were now Sister Sharon and Sister Michael, Sister Bridget, Sister Jean, Sister Marianne, and Sister Regina who both got to keep their own names since the order was dedicated to Mary, but in my thoughts, we all had our childhood names.

After lunch on Holy Saturday, we collected our change of undies and our toiletries – all put in a cloth bag with a drawstring. We took a textbook or two to study during free time. And we piled into the station wagon with Sister Michelle driving. Mother Evarista, Sister Biagina, Sister Mark, Sister Jeanne, Sister Patrick and Sister Faustina (me).

Mother Evarista settled herself and said to drive now. Sister Mark said, "Mother, wait. We don't have Sister James."

"Go ahead now and drive," Mother Evarista told Sister Michelle. She turned her head toward the rest of us in the second and third seats of the station wagon. "Sister James is staying with the house. We will go to the motherhouse now."

When she turned back to the front, we gave each other inquiring glances. This kind of thing had never happened before. We were always six.

No one seemed brave enough to ask the question so we drove silently to Blue Island. After a mile or two, Mother Evarista told Sister Patrick to start the rosary so that our puzzled thoughts were drowned out in repetitious Hail Marys.

Spending the night in our old quarters in the Aspirancy house was a treat. They only had three aspirants that year so we were able to squeeze in. We had one last practice with all the novices and aspirants in the high school chapel for our Easter anthems. Besides the stirring Alleluias, we would sing Regina Coeli Laetare, Queen of Heaven Rejoice.

Sister Michael, my old friend Rosie, snuck over to our dormitory after choir practice for a chat. She and I talked about her days at the Villa, dealing with Mother Leonard and the solemnity of her canonical year. Solemnity was not Rosie's natural bent. She was an athlete, graceful and at ease in her physical space. Her laissez faire attitude to work, to study, to life caused her to get more counseling hours than most of her peers. She looked to me to provide some reasoning behind the dictates of Mother Leonard and the Canonical rules but what could I tell her? You just keep your head down and try to do what the others are doing. When you get out in the parishes, teaching and doing parish work, you will have more freedom to be yourself.

She would look at me from under her white veil, and laugh and say "Sal, I don't know if I will last that long. I really don't." She never could call me Sister Faustina but I could call her Michael with ease because she was so athletic and androgynous. Simply the friend of my heart. Opposites attract.

Easter morning service was the joyous lifting of the heavy Lenten liturgies. With so many voices rising up, the Little Office sounded like angels were joining in. Although the Mass was long, we left the chapel with smiles and headed toward the cafeteria for breakfast. We were too many to fit in the motherhouse refectory that morning.

All of us novices and the three postulants sat together and caught up on our lives. One of the white-veil novices asked where Sister James was and a silence fell on our table because we didn't have an answer to this simple question.

"She stayed with the house," Sister Michelle said. Of course, that was not so. We didn't know it but Sister James' parents came to pick her up as soon as we left on Saturday. They must have brought her some clothes and she would have changed into them, leaving her habit on the bed, and then gathered up her books and toiletries and gone back to Tinley Park in the car with her mom and dad. Our first loss and the only one I was there to experience.

When we returned to Plainfield, nothing was said. Sister Evarista gave no explanations about Sister James and any questions about her absence were answered with a swift frown and a redirection such as "Sister, don't you have some classwork to do now?" Even Sister Biagina was silent. She had been through this before. When you were gone from the order, it was as if you never were there at all. Housekeeping tasks were sorted out so that James' assignments were given to the rest of us.

And that was that. A friend I had lived with since we were thirteen was just gone. Even without psychology classes, I knew this was not a healthy way to deal with loss. Bewilderment is soon followed by confusion, sadness and eventually resentment. I resented not being treated as an adult. I resented being hushed like a child, and I resented being forced to pretend that an entire friendship had not happened. Slate wiped clean.

And the worst part is that we were to believe that this pain should be subsumed into the sacrifices we must be willing to make as brides of Christ. Human connections were unimportant compared to your love and attachment to Jesus and his will. If you could not offer this sorrow into his arms, you were not worthy to be his bride.

Afraid of being found wanting, I bowed to the superior's will, not really convinced that it was Jesus' desire.

CHAPTER 30

Endings and Beginnings

WHEN THE SEMESTER was finished, all went to the motherhouse for the early summer retreat. Anxious to see and talk to my friend Rosie, now Sister Michael, I found an opportunity to whisper a time and a place to meet as we walked together, all eleven novices, both white veil and black veil, into the chapel.

After supper and dishwashing service, we went to the boarding school and climbed the two stories of outside stairs up to the flat roof. I searched out a clean place to sit. Sr. Michael wasn't worried about dirt and lounged against the chimney.

"Ro, did you know that James has gone?' I asked her. I still had faith that Rosie would know everything that was going on.

"No, Sal. What happened? No one told us anything. You know they wouldn't."

I related the story as I knew it, telling her how Sr. James had been so quiet and distant, spending time with a lay friend. And how she was gone when we came back from Easter.

"Jeez, Sal. That's the pits. Why did Colette leave?" Ro asked me.

And of course I had no answer. We didn't ask; she didn't tell. All that was left was confusion and regret and sadness. And the black curtain of obedient silence.

Sr. Michael and I talked for an hour or more about what was going on in our lives. She was trying to bend her independent nature to what we are told is God's will, as embodied in your superior's will. Michael was the oldest child in her family and used to having authority over her younger sisters and brother and also had freedom to come and go as she pleased. Way more than me, she found obedience to be impossible to understand and difficult to perform. She was always under the spotlight for various faults that she really didn't think were faults. I often wondered what kept her here in the convent but was grateful for her presence.

After breakfast the next morning, Mother Evarista called me into the parlor that I used to clean up on the second floor. She frowned so seriously that her brows came together and told me that Sr. Priscilla reported she heard young sisters talking into the night and she was concerned that we would not get our proper rest if we spent hours on the roof.

So we were found out. And I am sure that Sr. Michael was hearing the same thing from Mother Leonard, her novice mistress. I worried from afar that Sr. Michel would get dismissed since her fault would be more serious. As a first year novice she should have been more strictly sequestered than the second year novices. I fretted about her future but had no way to find out if she was forced out or forgiven.

CHAPTER 31

———— ❧ ————

Shorter Skirts

MOST NOTICEABLE IN our lives was the change in nuns' attire. We were received into the traditional garb: long habits, long sleeves, neck and head coverings and veil. Sometimes on the news we would see sisters in mid-calf habits without the wimple and coif, with a simple veil and hair showing! And the Franciscans who taught us at college were much more "modern" than the Mantellates. During the year we were in cloister, many of the college staff changed from a long skirt to a knee-length skirt and had a modified veil with the front part of their hair showing. All the young nuns in our classes wore the modified habit. I was jealous but thought it unlikely that we would be getting new duds anytime soon.

Well, I was wrong. During that summer, we had community meetings and discussion panels about the Pope's wishes for the church. Surprisingly, we were all given permission to shorten our skirts a few inches. Three below the knee was the password. Scissors were clicking as we raced to get our skirts raised before the first day of school. Sister Floriana and her crew produced a prototype of an acceptable new veil, a few inches below the shoulder instead of below the waist as our old ones were, and a white cuff around the face, no wimple or coif for those who wished to change. She was not happy but she obediently plied her needle and cut down the fine wool veils we wore, making two short veils out of one traditional veil.

The older sisters raised a ruckus and many refused to let their hair or their ankles show. In this instance, Mother Superior acted with compassion, allowing the older women to keep their traditional garb. No one was forced to change their habit. As time passed, several of the senior nuns adopted a more modern headgear after they saw how comfortable we were without the starchy pleated wimple and coif. Our new habits had a small, white, Peter Pan collar of soft polyester. You could easily wash it at night and it would be dry and ready to wear again in the morning.

Most surprising was seeing everyone's hair appear. Sr. Antoinette was indeed the fiery redhead I suspected her to be, although her red was now tempered with silver. Mother Evarista had black hair to match her eyebrows and Sr. Emilia showed the paler brown hair of Northern Tuscany. A few of the American sisters talked with us younger nuns about how to set their hair so it would have a little body. Ten or fifteen years of squashing their hair down under the coif had left them with lank tresses, no lift. It was amusing to see the first efforts at hairdressing. It was also amusing to listen to the sisters justifying their new-found vanity as trying to look professional, trying not to distract the people they serve from the message they try to deliver.

The driving sisters were probably the most grateful. They got back their peripheral vision and felt much more competent. Before the change, they had to swivel their heads left and right before making turns or lane changes. Now they could see all. And be safe. Sr. Concetta jumped right on the new fashion and even Sr. Ernesta adopted the new veil, if not the shorter skirt. Ernesta did all the purchasing and was asked a lot of questions by the Old Italian produce market people. They were curious about our habit changes. She mostly just told them to "ask the Popa."

Speaking of driving, Sr. Michael took it upon herself to teach me how to drive. Whenever her group of novices came out to the Plainfield house, she would get me into the car and have me drive around and around the little lake. Eventually she sent me out on the country road in front of the house. This road was usually very empty so we could go a long way before meeting another car. If a car came up behind us and started honking because I drove too slowly, Michael would stick her nunly head out of the window and motion them to go around, shouting "Student Driver" when they came even with us. In later years, I was grateful to her for giving me this skill – the driving, not the shouting.

CHAPTER 32

Going a Little Further

SUMMER WAS UPON us and the Rule was eased a bit. Sr. Andrea who was with us in our first year at the Villa broached a plan that the eleven of us black veiled and temporary vowed sisters should join her class of three sisters and all go to her cousin's cabin outside of St. Louis, Missouri and spend a week on vacation before the school year started. A chance to refresh and energize ourselves for the hard labor of teaching. The idea seemed totally impossible, even shocking. Nuns never had vacations, at least not in my experience. They were sometimes sent on retreat as a rest cure for emotional or psychological troubles but a vacation just for fun was not in the rules.

Miraculously, she applied for permission and she got it.

Mother Evarista and Sr. Biagina packed a bag apiece and went to the motherhouse for some community time with their sisters and the five of us made some calls to our homes, trying to gather up a few bathing suits for the week. We thought it would be better for the local population if they didn't know we were nuns when we went swimming. Silly of us. You always know when a person is a nun, even without the habit. Has something to do with lack of vanity and a receptive posture, poor fashion choices and sensible shoes.

Into two convent station wagons, fourteen giddy women piled, clutching our bags, some of them actual brown supermarket bags, filled with borrowed swimsuits and convent underwear. Nearly delirious with the scent of freedom, Sr. Mark insisted that the radio be turned on and we sang along with Aretha and Janis, and Paul Simon, faking it when we didn't know the words. After five or six cramped but happy hours of riding, we arrived at a small lake whose shores were dotted with a dozen vacation cabins. Several houses had hand-built piers that pushed out ten or fifteen feet into the clear water. Ours did not, but we had no boat so it made little difference.

The interior of the lake house was very plain: couches and chairs that did not match, several bedrooms with plain single beds or bunk beds and a dinky kitchen with only three chairs around a rickety Formica table. We didn't care a hoot about furniture. Simply being out from the all-seeing eye of a superior was a cause for dancing. Late August warmth called us outside like a siren's song. I went into the little bathroom and changed into the swimsuit in my carryall, coming out a little nervously to gauge the reaction of the other nuns.

"Wow! You are really white," said Sister Michelle. "Really white."

Yes I was. Never one to tan, my six years of being covered up left my arms and legs the color of alabaster. The only color I had was from freckles. And my hair. Smashed flat for many months but still shiny auburn.

As the others changed into swimsuits, the same verdict was laid upon all. Out we trooped into the afternoon sun to get something new – a tan.

St. Louis Zoo was scheduled for Thursday, and Tuesday night was bowling. My previous best game in bowling was 71 but since all were going, I went along. Sr. Andrea beat the pants off all of us with her 200 plus scores and Sr. Mark and Sr. Michael were close behind. The rest of us were just amateurs.

Such a large group of young women drew some attention from the bowling alley regulars. I could see young and middle-aged guys looking our way and chatting with each other, pointing out one or another of us. Beautiful Regina got the most attention.

Some fellows wandered over toward our lanes, casually, as if they were just heading toward the shoe rental. A tall Italian-looking guy and two others started talking to Sr. Michael, who was leaning on the back rail in her relaxed manner and she talked back. A policeman's daughter, she knew how to schmooze with men. Sr. Edward saw the knot of guys and moved into the conversation to make sure they were not bothering Michael. Maybe also to make sure Michael was not being disorderly. If anyone among us was going to be disorderly, it was Sr. Michael.

St. Louis had a marvelous zoo and that was our destination the next day. We provided an extra exhibit for the zoo visitors, walking along like a troop of penguins. We laughed and pointed and wandered around the zoo houses in a daze. So much freedom was an intoxicant. Sometimes a Catholic would come up to us and start to chat. Protestants kept their distance.

On this trip, prayers were left to each sister during the St. Louis week. I brought my Little Office and a few times I wandered around the wooded property surrounding the cabin for the purpose of reading the liturgy, but my interest was on baby squirrels and the fiddlehead ferns curling up from the forest floor. Not on Matins, Prime, and Tierce. I had no prayerfulness within me. More and more, when I prayed, I felt like I was simply talking inside my echoing head. Like the father of the boy inhabited by an evil spirit, I sometimes asked God to "help my unbelief." But no help arrived. Just silence. And boredom.

Soon the wild and wonderful week of freedom was over. We donned our short habits (I had shortened mine a good six inches while sitting on the cottage porch) and back we rode to our Plainfield house. Sr. Biagina greeted us with joy and was full of questions about our trip and our adventures. Mother Evarista did not want to hear too much. She pushed us back into the convent routine as rapidly as possible. This week of autonomy was an unusual event and Mother did not want us to think it would be happening often in future. We all got up the next morning, dressed and headed to chapel as if there had been no sweet days of liberty.

CHAPTER 33

———— ❧ ————

Heading into the Fields of the Lord

BESIDES OUR NEW, shorter habits, the Mantellate upper management decided we could – didn't have to, but could – go back to our birth names. So Sr. Mark was now Sr. Nancy, Sr. Jeanine was now Sr. Lois, and I was no longer Sr. Faustina but Sr. Sally Anne. I asked if I could be Sally Anne instead of my birth name of Sally Jane, just because it sounded more dignified and was given permission. Strange to find that permissions were flowing like milk and honey in that post-Vatican II era.

Although many of us in the white veil and black veil novice class were unaware or it, the "great exodus" had begun. Sisters ten and fifteen years older than us were leaving the order and going back to their family homes, becoming lay persons. Almost all of the Mantellates under the age of fifty, were American women. Some of them had been struggling for fifteen to twenty years to effect changes in the European model of convent life that they were governed by. Those teaching in the high school and in the parishes were fully aware of the changing attitudes among women religious and wanted to shake off the oppressive yoke of an eighteenth-century life style. Attending conferences with nuns of various orders – Franciscans, Benedictines, Maryknolls – showed our sisters how women religious could function in the church and in their convent lives. Too many attempts to get permission for changes in the way the schools and outlying convents were structured caused many to despair of being able to meet the needs of the school children or the parishioners. So a silent campaign of attrition transpired. Under the custom of silence, and being away from the motherhouse, we novices were not aware of the absentees.

For the Plainfield group there was another semester of schooling, summer school this time, and we were now in the month of August. The next item on our religious life schedule was to go to the motherhouse and get our work assignment. The entire order would come to Blue Island and have a special day of prayer and then be handed their mission for the next year.

Sisters were either excited or apprehensive, according to their personality. My assignment was for second grade a Seven Holy Founders Elementary School in Calumet Park. My superior there would be Sr. Gabriel whom I knew from my high school years. I was full of hope since I thought it would be terribly easy to teach second-graders. After all, I certainly knew the subjects much better than they did.

Sr. Katherine was sent to St. Bridget's in Hobart, Indiana, Sr. Nancy Anne was sent to St. Donatus in Blue Island, Sr. Nancy Hutchings went to Our Lady of Perpetual Help, which we called Perpet, and Sr. Lois was sent to the motherhouse in Blue Island. We all were sent to elementary schools which was probably because not one of us had taken any courses in pedagogy. We were only juniors in college-speak and had not yet declared any majors or minors. This type of unpreparedness was allowed in the Archdiocese of Chicago as long as the nuns were working toward a degree in education. Without this looseness, there would be few nuns teaching in the Catholic schools.

So, guilelessly, I made my farewells to my fellow-novices, packed my few possessions, and got a ride to Seven Holy Founders convent, three and a half miles away. Finally, after six years of training I would be a regular sister in a regular convent.

Changes appeared right and left of me. First was the absence of a cook. I had never cooked before but in the parish convents, sisters took weekly turns in the kitchen. Most convents had no cook or housekeeping sister. When you were up for cooking, you planned your week's meals, you bought the groceries, and you cooked them. Having absolutely no experience chopping and dicing, I tried to get ideas from the older sisters. They were unfailingly generous with their advice but not with the labor. Cook for the week is on her own. Breakfast was always simple and lunch was usually sandwiches or leftover casseroles since we had limited time away from the classroom. It was supper that tasked my talents. My fellow teachers were mostly kind about the burnt pork chops and the underdone lasagna. Lucky for me, I learned to make a really nice coffee cake ring filled with almond paste that helped smooth over my other culinary sins. The sisters also got the opportunity to offer up their sufferings for the poor souls in purgatory. And they knew my week as chef would soon be over and better meals were on the horizon.

Another difference in parish life is that the sisters usually say their prayers on their own time. We sang the Vespers and Compline at night but all the morning and afternoon hours and the rosary were yours to say when you were able to fit them in. That meant I could skip them and no one would know. Guilt was overlain by relief at not having to spend an hour or more reading the prayers that made no connection in my heart or mind.

In the couple of weeks before class started, I spent time decorating my classroom and preparing the stacks of books, readers, and workbooks that my fifty-two second-graders would be using. Sister Thomas was an old hand at this and guided me through this foreign territory. We had a large workroom in the lower level of the convent with several long tables and Sr. Thomas carted out the scissors and construction paper and glue. She showed me how to make borders for the bulletin boards and what type of pictures would best go along with the lessons. And lesson plans. I didn't know what one would look like but Sr. Thomas showed me the teacher's edition of the books. Usually there were lesson plans and materials lists already made for me. And I just copied them into my planner. On Sunday evenings, Sr. Gabriel who was also the principal of the school asked to see our lesson plans for the coming week. She often had something to add to mine but usually I passed the inspection.

CHAPTER 34

Teacher and Student

DAY AFTER LABOR Day I ate little breakfast because of the jitterbugging in my stomach. My second-graders were assembling on the playground. Soon the bell would ring and they would come line up in front of Sr. Sally Anne and we would walk into our classroom and I would start my teaching career.

They did line up and they did march into the classroom. I had already taped their names on their desks – alphabetical order, of course. They took a little while to find their seats. Standing at the front of the room in my shortened skirt and my shortened veil, I instructed them to put their notebooks and pencil cases in their desks as quietly as possible. When that little bit of business was over and all properties were stowed away, I asked them to rise and turn toward the flag. We started our day with something they already knew: the Pledge of Allegiance. When we were finished, I said, "Take your seats, please, children." And I introduced myself, writing my name on the blackboard. I dusted my hands of chalk and began the long first day of teaching.

These seven-year-olds were a strange breed to me. They were cute in their blue Catholic school uniforms and full of curiosity. I had no experience with shepherding little ones, being the youngest in my family but they were, in general, well-behaved and eager to have something to do. Soon I learned to overfill my lesson plans because nothing took as long as I planned. We would be finished with math fifteen minutes before the clock said we should. Same with reading, social studies, spelling, and religion. Even bathroom break went by faster than I expected.

Gaps in our schedule were filled with singing. If I couldn't think of anything for fifty-two seven-year-olds to do, we sang. This class of 1968 learned to sing in Italian, French, Latin, Spanish, and German. And English. We sang "Sur La Pont D'Avignon", "O Tannenbaum," "Milan Brucia," "Cielito Lindo," "Tantum Ergo," and more. Perhaps they lacked a little rigor in their math or spelling but they could really sing.

The need for a teaching certificate was still hanging over my head. The way to reach it was to attend college classes in the evenings after teaching all day. Three or four of us would get into the convent car and drive to downtown Chicago to Loyola University for night classes. I took two courses per semester and in the spring semester I got permission to take a voice class at DePaul. Since the convent was keeping me in the position of choir director, I needed to learn how to help the choir produce good tones.

Walking from Loyola to DePaul took a very few minutes and the beauty of Chicago's architecture kept me excited. Every building has some little gargoyle or Corinthian column or glass and stone detail that made it distinct from every other building and my training in custody of the eyes was lost when I was downtown. My eyes also fell up groups of sailors since the Great Lakes Naval Station was not far north of the Loop. In winter, the fellows walked around in fine blue-black wool uniforms with bell bottom pants and square collars on their backs. In the summer, the outfits changed to pressed white with a knotted blue kerchief. I didn't think of them as military or fighting men; they just looked so cute. Smiling to myself, I wondered if I could have one of those.

The bubbly effects of my relative freedom were a new feeling for me. The old rule of never going anywhere secular without a companion sister was being ignored. When I finished my class at

Loyola and headed toward DePaul for music, there was no one else enrolled at DePaul so I walked there alone. The two-by-two laws were vanquished. Complete poverty was relaxed by the issuing of a little pocket money so one could buy a cup of coffee or have a dime for a phone call. In the mission houses, we no longer were obliged to ask permission for every little thing. If you needed more socks or underwear or typing paper, you just took what was necessary and didn't bother the superior with your requests. The superior was busy with her own work – teaching her classes, doing administrative work as school principal, taking on any tasks sent to her by the parish priest and supervising her company of sisters. She was much busier than our postulant and novice mistresses whose only task was to keep us under scrutiny and make assessments of our worthiness.

Still, there were limits to our new personal freedom and I learned of them the hard way.

CHAPTER 35

Professional Women

ROSIE, SR. ROSEMARY now, called and asked if I could go home with her during the Easter break. She wanted to visit her mother and there was a lady whom her mother knew who needed some household help. Sr. Rosemary proposed that she and I could spend a day at this lady's home and help her with cleaning or cooking or whatever would be best. Sounded great to me. One thing I was pleased to finally be doing was helping people, through teaching or parish projects, or home visitations. This visit needed Sr. Gabriel's permission and she kindly gave it to me.

Sr. Rosemary came by and picked me up since I didn't drive yet in the city. We drove to her mother's home and stayed there a few hours, eating the wonderful food that Mrs. Bradaric was always making. Then we said goodbye and drove to the other lady's house in Flossmoor, about 15 miles away.

With a bag of old pants and shirts in hand, we rang the bell. A small Italian women came to the door and was so happy to see two sisters on her stoop. She kept saying, "Come in, come in. God bless you, sisters, for coming to see me." Leaning on her cane, she led us down the hall into the living room.

We told her we were sent her to help her with anything that she needed done: cleaning, cooking, laundry, washing windows. We were hers for the day. We both changed into the old clothes Ro had brought. It was a little strange to look at each other in pants and shirts, but I felt like a modern religious who dresses for the job. I don't know what Sr. Gabriel might have felt if she had seen us.

Rosemary looked around and saw dishes in the sink. "Sal, why don't you do the dishes and I'll sweep the floor and vacuum in the living room," she said. And so we did. We dusted, we windexed the mirrors, we cometed the tub and sink. After a couple of hours, the little apartment was looking quite shiny.

We went into the living room where the lady was watching TV with her little dog on her lap. "What else can we do for you, dear?" Rosemary asked.

"Oh, this was so kind of you. I don't want to take up any more of your time. You young ladies have more important things to do than work in my old house," she said shyly.

"No ma'am, we do not. We are yours for as long as you need us," I spoke this time, having lost my shyness in the midst of scrubbing her house.

"Well, I do have one other thing that needs to be done, My son, Jimmy, was going to do it for me but he is in the hospital now with pneumonia and can't work for a while" she said.

"Just name it, dear. We are here," Rosemary told her.

"My bedroom is so dark and sad, especially since my husband passed and I sleep all alone. My Jimmy went and bought me some paint – a nice light yellow – so it would look happier. Do you think you could paint it for me since Jimmy can't do it now?" she asked us, looking up from her cavernous floral armchair like a tiny gnome on a peony blossom.

I looked at Rosemary and she looked at me. At least we were dressed for painting and wouldn't go home with sunny yellow dots on our black habits. We found everything needed on the bedroom dresser. Why didn't I notice this pile of painting supplies when I dusted in here? Rosemary told me to take the brush and start cutting in while she moved the furniture away from the walls. She would use the roller for the big areas since she was stronger than I. Such a little room, it only took two hours and the dirty vanilla walls were covered with sunny yellow. We had the windows open to let out the paint smell. The lady of the house came in when we called her. Carrying her dingy white poodle in her arms, she was amazed at the change a little fresh paint made.

"Thank you, thank you, girls. You've done so much for me. I don't know how to thank you" she said.

"It's nothing," Rosemary told her. "We enjoyed doing it. We'll just change and get out of your way here."

Rose and I took turns in the tiny bathroom, getting out of our pants and cotton shirts and putting on our short habit and veil. When we both were finished we went into the living room to say goodbye to our host.

"Mother of God," she said when she saw us in our habits again. "I forgot you were even nuns. You walked around in trousers all day. I started to think you were just girls from Family Services. Sisters, I would never have asked you to paint my walls if I had remembered you were nuns."

She was so abashed. We rushed to tell her that this is why we came to visit her and we told her how much we enjoyed doing this. Most of our work was in books and some physical labor was a great change, we said. As we hurried down the hall to the front door, she pressed a wrinkled paper bag of Italian cookies into my hand. I said, "No, no" because I didn't want her to deprive herself of the sweets and also because they were pretty crumpled and broken but she prevailed and we had to take the cookies as her thank you to us.

After we tumbled into the car, Rosemary said to me, "That was fun, Sal, but more than I expected. Now we have to go home and make up all those prayers we missed."

Mid-bite of a broken cookie, I blinked at her in surprise. Somehow I had passed the whole day without once thinking of prayer or the Little Office or the rosary. I was ashamed but the idea was planted and growing inside my head that I didn't need those things. I didn't feel more fulfilled or closer to God when I say the prayers than when I omitted the prayers. The idea that no one was listening because no one was out there started to solidify in my head. Unbelief had been an enveloping cloud that I dragged around for a long time but my desire to be part of the convent family kept the cloud tamped down. While the bridegroom Jesus did not have the power to keep me in religious life, the bonds between my sisters and myself did have that power. And the thought that I might do some good for some people had that same power. My interior motivation was a lamp that I kept hidden even from my own inspection. I needed to stay in my safe situation until I was strong enough to smother that lamp and move on.

Later in the month our convent at Seven Holy Founders had a visit from Mother Angela. Formerly my eighth-grade History teacher, she was our Mother Superior now. Mother Angela was a hybrid: both Italian and American, and took an intellectual approach to most issues. The Italian faction didn't trust her completely, and neither did the young American faction. Mother Angela was not a fence-sitter but one could not predict which side of an issue would be hers. I liked her and felt liked in return. Stopping by our Seven Holy Founders convent, she had a talk with Sr. Gabriel and then Sr. Gabriel came to my room and told me Mother Angela would like to talk with me. I smiled and said I will be right there.

In my short habit and my short veil, I sailed into the parlor and greeted Mother Angela. She said good morning to me and asked me to have a seat.

"Sister, where did you go last Saturday?" she questioned.

"Mother, Sr. Rosemary asked permission for me to accompany her on a visit to her mother's house. You know her mama, she misses Rosemary so much. Sr. Gabriel gave us permission to go visit her.

"And what else did you do Saturday?"

Smiling at the expected approval of our good deed, I told Mother Angela about the widowed friend of Rosemary's mother, and how we two went there and cleaned her house since she was doing poorly and her son was in hospital. And I told about how quickly we painted the little bedroom and how happy the lady was. I should have noticed the darkening look on Mother Angela's face as I prattled on.

"So, Sister Sally Anne, it was just as I heard. You and Sister Rosemary went to a private home and painted the walls! What kind of precedent do you think that sets? Can you see the people of the parish calling the convent and asking if the sisters could come over and help clean out their garage, or mow their lawn or help them put up the storm windows? Sister, we are professional women and we need to keep up our status in the community as professional women. We need to be seen as a source for guidance and support by the families, not as another source of unpaid manual labor.

I didn't mention that we had been paid by the gratitude in that lady's smile and the tin of broken Italian cookies.

"And your habits, Sister. Did you get paint on your habits? The habit is a holy garment and is not to be disrespected," Mother Angela said.

"Oh, Mother, we were very careful to keep out habits out of the paint, not a spot on them," I assured her, not adding that we carefully folded our habits and changed into civvies – civilian clothes. That knowledge shared could possibly result in apoplexy.

Mother Angela soon left after my apologies and her judgment that I was reasonably repentant and would not embarrass the convent in future. She advised me to pray on my actions and I went to my bedroom and sat on the bed, pondering what just happened. Two sisters in religion, Rosemary and myself, went into the world and assisted an elderly woman who had no one to help her. We practiced the virtue of charity, as I saw it, but were reprimanded for that because we did not keep our distance from one of God's creatures. I hated getting in trouble but taking the longer view, I could not see how to avoid trouble since the philosophy at work in my superiors didn't parse in my mind. An action that was an offense to the higher authority was a virtue in my mind. So how would I ever discern what was expected?

CHAPTER 36

────────── ✣ ──────────

Lazy, Crazy, Hazy Days of Summer

JUNE FINALLY ARRIVED and the final tasks of teaching took all of our interest: giving the diocesan tests to our kids, averaging grades and writing our report cards, conferencing with parents. Happily, none of my little ones failed to move up to third grade. Once we had organized our classrooms, piled the textbooks up on the shelves and cleaned the desks and chairs of grimy fingerprints and stray crayon marks, we shut the doors and headed to the motherhouse for the annual retreat.

Five days of silence, prayer, meditation, spiritual reading did not appeal to me. Also, I knew we would each have an interview with Mother Angela to assess our progress. If I told her the truth, my spiritual state would be seen as appalling to her. My faith in God was depleted. Believing the story of Christianity was no longer possible for me and especially the facets of the Catholic faith that were church doctrine but were not in the Bible. Dogma such as the immaculate birth of Mary and the assumption of Mary's body into heaven after her death, forbidding women to fully participate in the church. But I was delighted to be able to see my fellow junior sisters and the six who were in the class after mine.

After the five days passed, I started the summer semester at Loyola downtown. Trigonometry was on the list but my concentration was very thin. Most of my hours downtown were spent wandering the canyons of the Loop and worrying over my future. Submitting to the Rule and praying five hours a day when I couldn't believe in God, the basis of the prayers, was becoming intolerable.

I should have gone to my house superior, Sr. Gabriel, and talked but she and I had only developed a passing relationship. Her perfect posture and her habit of retreating to her room at all possible moments kept her distant from personal contact. I sensed that she wanted her house to be consistently trouble-free, and her sisters to be obedient and quiet. Bringing my doubts and questions to her would just upset her and I didn't think she would have any helpful advice for me. Deep down I knew the answer was to leave. And I was closer and closer to being able to take that step into the future.

So, three days a week a car left the convent, filled with nuns who were working on their teaching degrees. We each had two or three classes to attend and all stayed downtown until the last class was finished. Then we pile back into the station wagon headed back home to the convent. I wanted to talk with my sisters about what I thought of as a decision – I would leave at the end of the semester – but long training had conditioned me to silence on this subject. My sisters all gave the impression that they intended to stay in this religious life so I hesitated to thrust my troubles into what I saw as their calm and Christ-centered lives. The idea that many of them were struggling with thoughts of leaving at the same time never came to mind.

All that last summer, I practiced scenarios in my mind: what would it be like if I stayed in the convent, taught school, zoned out during prayers and tacitly agreed to the life dedicated to work and sacrifice? On the other hand: what would it be like if I left the convent and my sisters of these seven years, went home to my family, got a job or continued my college work, got a boyfriend (!) and had sex and got married? I was nearly twenty-one; perhaps I was too old to find a husband. But leaving seemed more and more attractive than staying. Our little coterie of sisters had been dispersed to various parishes and that support in numbers was no longer accessible. The sisters in my mission parish, though not unkind, were distant and preoccupied with their own problems. The only one who took time to talk with me was Sister Thomas.

Thomas was gruff and unpolished, and definitely not one of the ruling class. In a sidelong manner, she gave me many pointers on how to keep our jobs as cooks, teachers, students, and nuns in balance. When I finally told her I thought I had to go home, she didn't act surprised.

"I can drive you home, you know. Anytime you want. I have the car keys. We'll just slip out after evening prayers and I can drive you to your mom's house. Just tell me when," she offered.

While it was kind of Thomas to be so voluntary, still I was not ready to make that move. Having actually achieved the habit and the role of a sister had been my goal for so long. And now, to find my faith had slipped away as water slipping from a pot with a hole near the bottom, my life as a sister, barely begun, must be abandoned.

Needing advice, I wrote to Professor Goicoechea. He had been in seminary and left. He could help me sort this out and give me the courage to leave. He wrote back that he would be in Chicago on a day that I had class and we could meet at Loyola, his alma mater. He was teaching in Toronto at Brock University but often returned to the states.

On the appointed day I skipped my Trig class and met David in Loyola's Lewis Towers off Michigan Avenue. With the usual palpitations that he caused my heart, I waited in the lounge for him to arrive. Young students were coming in and going out, tossing their books on tables, throwing heavy backpacks on the carpet. Finally David rushed into the lounge, a few minutes late, and looked around till he saw me sitting there with my trig book open on my lap. Smiling warmly, he came over and raised me from the chair and gave me a hug.

"Let's go upstairs. We'll find a room where we can talk," he said. His black hair was disheveled from the breeze off the lake and his smile was just the medicine I needed at that moment.

We took the stairs and wandered down the hall until he saw a row of empty classrooms. Guiding me by the elbow into that room, we sat and talked for a while. I poured out my woes; he listened. When I finished, I asked, "What shall I do, David? I have to leave, don't I?"

He didn't answer but wrapped his arms around me. I leaned into him because this was where I had always wanted to be. But the incongruity of my clothing and my position kept my mind jumbled. My years of convent training told me this was not right. I finally pulled away, gathering my books and trying to speak in a relaxed voice.

"David, the car will be leaving soon. I must get over to the car park or I'll be stranded here in the city all night," I said. While my body worked at packing up my belongings, my head and heart where both whirling like a storm of maple helicopters. This had been a crazy day. So many sins to count if I still bought into the bookkeeping of sins. And I knew that I would soon be going home. The rest of my problem would only be logistics.

CHAPTER 37

———— ✧ ————

Flight by Midnight

BACK IN MY narrow convent bed, my roiling mind finally allowed the possibility of leaving convent life to come to the forefront. To continue as the bride of Christ was dishonest for one who no longer believed in the Father, the Son, and the Holy Spirit. Even though I paid for my keep with my labors as teacher, cook, cleaner, I was the wolf in sheep's clothing.

I resolved to go home but I didn't have the inner courage to face my superior and explain myself. So, I waylaid Sr. Thomas and asked her if she had been serious about driving me home. She said she was so now I had to see if I had a home to go home to.

Next Visiting Sunday, when my parents and I were alone in one of the parlors, I nervously asked them if they would mind if I left the convent and came home. Mama was the first to say, "Of course, we have room for you. We always wanted you to come home but you seemed so happy here."

"Are they treating you bad here?" my father asked. His fatherly spirit of protection had been stymied by the hierarchy of the convent. He didn't understand it, having been brought up as a Methodist, but he was ready to protect his daughter at all costs.

"No, Papa. No one is treating me badly, but I don't think this is the way I want to live the rest of my life. I came in here when I was thirteen. I knew nothing about the world or about life. And now I am twenty and I don't see this life of chastity and obedience as my path. I want to come home and get a job and find my own life. Maybe marry, maybe not. Is it okay with you and Mama?" I said

"Baby, I just wish you have come to this six months earlier. I just built a new house and I would have built another bedroom for you. As it is, you will have to share with your grandma," was his practical reply.

So it was decided. With shaking hands, I gathered together what few things I had that were mine: some cards from friends, letters, a little silver locket that Rosie had given me engraved with her name. Placing these in my old footlocker along with a couple of books, I asked Sr. Thomas when she thought we could go.

"Let's do this tomorrow night, around eleven. Everyone should be asleep by then. I'll take your footlocker down to the garage when everyone is in chapel for Vespers and put it in the back of the station wagon. Then we will drive out quietly," she said.

"Right. I'll meet you there. And thanks," I answered. Again, a flock of butterfly ballerinas was tripping around in my midsection, but I knew I had to do this and she was willing to help.

Eleven o'clock sharp, I walked down the stairway to the garage, got in the car next to Sr. Thomas, and looked at her. She could see the struggle of emotions in my face.

"You really want to go?" she asked one last time.

"I have to," I told her.

And she started the station wagon and quietly rolled out of the garage. Above us, on the second floor, I noticed a light had come on in one of the sisters' bedroom. Sr. Gabriel's head appeared through a parted curtain. She looked down upon the scene: something unauthorized was going on and she likely had a good idea of what it was. But she did nothing to stop us.

After seven years of this safe and sheltered and stifling life, Sr. Thomas drove me back into the world.

"Writing, in making the world light — in codifying, distorting, prettifying, verbalizing it — approaches blasphemy."

John Updike, Self-Consciousness

Epilogue

Did she get the sailor?

Yes, I did. Within three months of my exodus, a real, live U.S. Navy sailor came to my house and asked me to go out on a date.

I spent my first weeks out of the convent searching for a job and began working in downtown Chicago as a receptionist. I didn't have much in the way of employable skills, other than cleaning, so I felt lucky to get on the Rock Island train every morning in Tinley Park, travel to LaSalle Street station, walk several blocks to my job which was mostly working a plug-through switchboard and answering phones with "Massachusetts Mutual Life Insurance Company. How may I help you?" In a month or so, their bookkeeper left so I got to move up a desk.

The days of the miniskirt were upon us and Mama took me shopping in that first week home. We bought four or five outfits for me to wear to work. And the skirts were the shortest ever. Walking the bridge over the Chicago River in wintertime was a cold, cold moment for us fashion plates in our miniskirts.

Mama and Grandma Anna had a little distress when I refused to go to church with them. They could not believe I meant it when I said I no longer believed so I mostly said I was tired of church and had many years of daily masses stocked up so I could stay home for a long time before they would run out.

The sailor wanted to marry right away but I said let's hold off for a while and get to know each other. Even I knew that having your first date at the age of twenty-one was a little odd. A year later we married and made our first home in Norfolk outside the Naval Base. Soon we were sent to New London, Connecticut and had a son there at the submarine base hospital.

All through my life I found that people, on learning that I had been a nun, want to ask why I left the convent. Most of the time I give them the easy answer. I entered at fourteen, still in puberty, and stayed until I was twenty-one. The adult part of my self finally was starting to emerge and after seeing those cute sailors on the streets of Chicago, I began to think of other options that I might take. I took the coward's way out instead of sharing the true reason I gave up the safe and sheltered life of a Catholic nun.

The truth is I simply no longer believed in god. The philosophies and religions that I had studied as part of my course material showed me that it was not people who were created by god but the gods were created by people because we need something larger than ourselves to cling to. The variety of gods supports my thesis. Greeks had their array of deities, so did Icelanders, Indians, and Arabs. And they made them because they needed support in the dangers of living. As we learned more about the universe, the insignificance of humans became evident. We rightly felt small and defenseless in the face of space and the forces of nature on our own planet. And to counter that people have created gods: gods who will give them the good harvest or the victory over their enemies, gods who will make their wombs fertile and keep their children safe, especially gods who love them and care for them and have counted the hairs upon their heads.

But the truth is, gods do not keep us safe, well fed, victorious or fertile. The religions of the world revealed themselves to be "smoke and mirrors" in my eyes and I had to leave that life.

All that is left to me of the convent years are the good values of kindness and hard work, the Latin songs I sing while vacuuming, the friendships of my sisters who have also come home, and these mostly happy memories of my young days.

The irony of life is inescapable so it should surprise no one that my second husband was a Lutheran lay minister, After Levi and I married, I spent my Sundays going to not one but two Lutheran services every Sunday, often directing the choir or playing the piano and organ. In our rural area, churches often don't have enough members to support a full-time pastor so they share one. And the pastors are often bi-vocational, meaning they have a regular job in addition to pastoring. Levi's profession was barbering which suited his pastoral work well. He conversed with people all day, sometimes doing a little pastoral advising, sometimes getting some fuel for his next sermon. After his death from melanoma, I still attended two services, employed as the organist for their liturgy. The job kept me in practice and made me feel that Levi was still close by. Now that arthritis has made my playing unacceptable, I finally get to stay home on Sunday mornings and be the "unchurched" person that I am.

How could a Lutheran minister marry an atheist? Because he was such an exceptionable human being. Levi encompassed my unbelief and firmly believed that his love would win me a place in heaven. So often I told him that he was wrong but he didn't waiver. If he was right, he would pull me up to heaven. That was the plan. After Levi died of cancer, I ordered the headstone. On his side it says Mahatma, meaning great soul. On my side it says "Pull me up, darlin'." If he was right, he will do that. If I am right, we will simply become stardust.

In the summer of 2016 we ex-sisters gathered together in Joliet, Illinois for a weekend reunion. Some of us had not met in person for 48 years and the possibility that we would not have anything in common but memories worried me. When we finally had all gathered and started to talk, the past 48 years vanished. The same girls we remembered were still inside the women we saw across the table. But the girlish insecurities and petty jealousies were gone and each woman was the better, wiser, more tolerant version of the same girl we had lived with. Not one was bitchy, narrow-minded, or greedy. And for that, the Mantellate Sisters should be proud. Their formation efforts turned out strong and loving women. The majority became teachers, some accountants, nurses, social workers. Two actually stayed in the convent but were unable to attend the gathering due to commitments.

A common theme of the reunion was how much each ex-sister treasured her years in the convent, not as time wasted but as time spent growing from naïve girlhood to self-actuated adulthood. For two nights and two days, we talked and laughed and drank wine and shared stories that some remembered and others had forgotten. Denise recalled that one of my tasks was to bring breakfast up on a tray to the parlor for the priest who came to say mass for us at the Villa Santa Maria. I had forgotten that completely. More so, she remembered me coming down the stairs to the kitchen with the empty tray and telling her that Father had said a strange thing to me. He said he had a new pair of roller skates and asked me if I had a key. She understood what I recounted but I did not. That was few years before Melanie's Roller Skate Song came out.

Reuniting showed what a slippery snake memory is. People and places are not solid. They slip in and out, changing dates and places. Significance grows and wanes. So I agree with John Updike, "what I have written here strains to be true, but it is, nevertheless, not true enough." Others who lived the same moments will have different accounts and I hope someday to read them. These moments and memories made us the people we are today. No regrets, no remorse. Just a smile of recognition for the girls we were: sincere, altruistic and well-intentioned without exception.

"WE REMEMBER PAST MOMENTS…AND WE INVENT CONTINUITY WITH THE EARLIER SELF, BUT IT IS FICTION. WE ARE ONLY WHO WE ARE RIGHT NOW, AND THE STABILITY AND CONTINUITY OF THE SELF IS A COMFORTING ILLUSION."

JOHN LANCHESTER "FAMILY ROMANCE"

72254243R00113

Made in the USA
Columbia, SC
15 June 2017